Managing Negative Emotions

Stop Anger, Stress, Anxiety, and Other Intrusive Feelings From Controlling Your Life and Achieve Inner Peace

Andrew Tenny

1

Table of Contents

Introduction

Do you find yourself feeling worried, angry, or frustrated more frequently than you would like? Maybe you are feeling negative, but you do not understand why. More importantly, what do you do when you are feeling negative? Do you distract yourself to avoid the way that you feel? Maybe, you allow yourself to become overwhelmed by it.

Emotions are an inherent aspect of the human condition. We all experience emotions, though how we handle them can vary from person to person. The emotions that are most challenging to deal with are our negative emotions. We tend to avoid dealing with them. Emotional well-being comes when we can accept and manage the emotions we are experiencing.

Having worked in the mental health field for over twenty years and having practiced meditation for just as long, I have come a long way in learning how to embrace and learn from all feelings that I experience. I have learned that all emotions have their place and that there are no emotions that I should not be experiencing. I have learned to use all my emotions to gain information about what I need to become happier in my life.

It was this understanding that inspired me to write this book. Too many people suffer because they do not deal directly with their emotions, which is not surprising. As a culture, we have become too distracted by our digital and fast-paced lives. We have lost touch with what we are experiencing within ourselves.

In this book, you will learn about the most common negative emotions experienced, what causes them, their symptoms, and how you can cope with them. Additionally, you will learn about what emotions are, their nature, and the value they provide. My wish is that you learn to use your emotions to empower you rather than try to evade them.

Chapter 1:
What Are Emotions?

We often over-complicate things by breaking them down and treating them as separate entities. For example, a mechanic may focus on the different parts of a car when trying to understand what the problem is.

Similarly, a doctor may run different tests and examine different parts of the body to determine what is causing a malady. While such approaches serve a purpose, they can also keep us from appreciating a more holistic view of things. It keeps us from understanding the bigger picture, which is true with our emotions.

When it comes to our emotions, we focus on their parts, leading us to either embrace or vilify them. If we experience happiness, excitement, or peace, we embrace these feelings and enjoy the experience. If we feel sadness, anger, or fear, we succumb to, deny, or suppress the feeling. Just as a mechanic or a doctor, we have focused on our parts and judged whether our parts are acceptable. If we take a deeper look at emotions, we will find that they are a natural aspect of us and that they serve us.

A misunderstanding of emotions has been fostered over many generations. For years, we were taught that men need to be strong and not show emotions and that expressing emotions is a sign of weakness. At the same time, we were taught that women were emotional by nature.

The consequence of these distorted views is that males tended to suppress their feelings while women were not taken seriously. Thankfully, these views have begun to be challenged by more recent generations. However, these views still are retained by many of us.

A Deep Dive Into Emotions

The human body, as with everything else in this universe, is made of energy. Energy is the foundation of everything that we experience. Let us use your finger, for example. Your finger is composed of skin, tissue, bone, blood vessels, and tendons. Each of these components is made of cells. Cells are made of various intercellular structures.

If we dive deeper into these intercellular structures, we will eventually find molecules. In turn, these molecules are made of atoms. Atoms are made of subatomic particles. If we take a deep dive into these subatomic particles, what we would eventually come to is a non-physical realm, a realm of pure energy.

Whether we are talking about a tree, a brick, or a finger, they are all expressions of energy. Though the idea that energy can take on a physical form may seem strange, we experience it each day, not just in our bodies but in our technology.

Electromagnetic energy cannot be detected, yet they make it possible for us to listen to the radio, use a cellphone, or take an x-ray of a broken bone. When you watch television, you are looking at information that was transmitted from far away, reassembled, and projected on your television screen as an image.

As with the television set, your body, thoughts, and emotions are all different expressions of the same energy. When you experience an emotion, you are experiencing just one of the infinite expressions of energy.

A Different Perspective of Emotions

Since emotions are energy forms, we should learn how to manage that energy rather than allow it to manage us. Additionally, managing emotions would be easier if we remember that emotions are just expressions of energy.

A battery has a positive and negative terminal. We do not view the positive terminal as "good" and the negative one as being "bad." It would be valuable if we could similarly treat our emotions. The reason for this is that emotions are neither "good" nor "bad." We experience them as being "either-or" because that is what we were taught to believe. There is nothing in life that has any inherent meaning to it. Rather, it is we who create the meaning of our experiences. In truth, our emotions are no more "good" or "bad" than are the terminals of a battery.

A battery works by conducting energy, storing it, and then releasing it. Similarly, we conduct, store, and release emotions. At least, this is how it is supposed to be. In this book, you will learn how to make this your reality.

Chapter 2:
An Intelligent Universe

I t was previously stated that the fundamental nature of the universe is energy. However, the energy that I speak of is not like the energy that we commonly think of. The energy that I am speaking of is intelligent in that it can think.

Though this statement may seem strange to some, you only need to look at this world to see examples of this. The seasons change, following the same pattern with predictability. The tides rise and all. The planets follow a specific orbit. Living beings are constantly dying and being born. The body contains trillions of cells that perform innumerable physiological processes that ensure our survival. Though each cell has its specialized function, they communicate with each other and support each other's existence.

It is this same intelligent energy that flows through us. Among the different ways that we experience this energy are our thoughts and emotions. Thoughts and emotions arise from the same energy; however, we experience them in different ways.

Thoughts are experienced linguistically, meaning that they seem to speak to us, while emotions are experienced through feelings. However, both emotions and thoughts provide us with the same information. If you are experiencing negative thoughts, you will experience negative emotions. Conversely, if you are experiencing negative emotions, you will also experience negative thoughts.

You can change how you feel by changing your thoughts, and you can change your thoughts by changing how you feel. This mirroring of thoughts and emotions provides us with an important tool for personal growth. The reason for this is that many of our challenges are due to subconscious thoughts; thoughts that we are not aware of. We can connect with our subconscious thoughts if we pay attention to what we are feeling.

The Hierarchy of Emotions

Energy takes on different forms based on its frequency. Low frequencies lead to denseness, while high frequencies lead to spaciousness. An example of this is water. When the atoms in a water molecule vibrate at low frequencies, water takes on the form of ice. When the atoms vibrate rapidly, it leads to water taking on the form of water vapor.

The energy frequencies of our emotions have the same effect. Depression or sadness has a low frequency, leaving us feeling heavy. Gratitude, appreciation, and love have high frequencies, which leave us feeling light, and in some cases, like we are floating on air.

The following is the hierarchy of emotions. We will begin with the bottom of the hierarchy and work upward:

Apathy: Apathy is a state where there is the suppression of emotions; we lose our connection with them. Because of this, it can be said that apathy is the suppression of energy.

Shame: Shame is an emotional energy that is caused by holding a negative view of ourselves. Since thoughts and emotions reflect each other, the emotion of shame causes us to attract thoughts that have a similar nature. When this occurs, it reinforces the feeling of shame. A closely related emotion to shame is depression.

Guilt: Guilt is one step above shame and is caused when we recognize that we behaved in a manner that has caused harm to others or ourselves. Additionally, there is a concern about how others will feel about us because of our actions.

If I steal something from another, my actions are not consistent with how I want to be seen as a person. My guilt expresses the inconsistency between my behavior and how I want to think about myself.

While shame shows up as not liking who we are, guilt is a reminder that how we conducted ourselves was not aligned with how we see ourselves. Guilt is a message telling you that you must change how

9

you perceive and treat others. If guilt causes you to improve how you relate to others, it will have done its job.

Grief: The emotion of grief occurs when we experience a sense of loss. The loss can range from the death of a loved one, the loss of a job, or the loss of independence due to a disability. Grief is deeply personal, and everyone can express grief differently.

Fear: Fear is the anticipation of loss; we fear losing something important to us. Fear is one step above grief because we often feel immobilized when we are in grief. However, the emotion of fear can work both ways. It can stop you in your tracks or lead to taking action that will prevent a loss. A closely related emotion to fear is anxiety.

Anger: Anger can be a response to an actual loss or the threat of one. Anger is a step higher in energy level than fear. While fear can leave you feeling immobilized, anger can motivate you to take action.

The emotions that were just discussed are found at the lower end of the energy hierarchy because they share common characteristics. All of these emotions cause us to focus on ourselves. When experiencing any of these emotions, we are focused on the fear of loss or how others may perceive us. For this reason, these emotions are ego-based.

It is these characteristics that create "negative emotions." These emotions create a sense of limitation in us. It goes back to what was stated before; we complicate our lives by breaking things down and treating them as separate entities. In the case of negative emotions, we see ourselves as being separate and vulnerable to loss, which creates fear. It is our fear that lowers our energy.

The next emotions we will explore are located midway and toward the top of the hierarchy. Because these emotions cause us to pay less attention to our ego-based minds, they have a higher vibrational frequency, which causes us to feel more vital and empowered.

Satisfaction: The lowest of the more empowering emotions, satisfaction is experienced when the fear of loss has been temporarily abated. Because we are not focusing on our fear of loss, our attachments to those things outside ourselves are reduced. For example, I may experience fear of a relationship breakup.

10

My fear lies with what I will lose if that person leaves me. This fear occurs because I have formed an emotional attachment to this person. If this person decides they want to stay in the relationship, my fear will subside because the fear of loss has been eliminated. Because the fear of loss has been eliminated, I feel less emotionally attached to this person.

To clarify, when I speak of emotional attachment, I am not referring to my caring for this person. Rather, I am referring to my emotional dependency on them.

Happiness: The emotion of happiness is a step above satisfaction in that it has a higher frequency. In happiness, not only is there no focus on the fear of loss, but there is also hope or anticipation of a desirable event.

As with all emotions, happiness is unstable and fleeting if its source is grounded in something outside us, such as a new relationship, acquiring material goods, or a vacation.

The happiness most of us experience is contingent upon the circumstances of our life matching up to our liking. When this occurs, the happiness we experience will be unstable. Since change is a constant in life, our circumstances are bound to change. To enjoy a more stable form of happiness, its source must come from within us.

Joy: The emotion of joy is similar to happiness, except it is experienced more strongly. As with happiness, joy is also unstable, even more so than happiness. The reason for this is the same as in happiness. If our joy is due to an external event, that event will, at some point, change. True joy can only occur when it is based on something within us, such as personal growth and achievement.

Gratitude: The emotion of gratitude has a higher frequency than joy because this emotion tends to be more enduring. Gratitude is an emotion that is expressed when we receive a form of benefit. It is a higher emotion than joy because it causes us to focus on something outside of ourselves.

If a person gives me a gift of money, which I really could use, I will experience gratitude toward that person. Because my focus is on the other person, it is not going to my ego-based mind. It is this outward focus that gives this emotion a higher vibration.

Appreciation: Appreciation is a higher emotion than gratitude because it involves an even more outward focus. Gratitude is expressed when we receive a benefit, so it depends on us receiving something. On the other hand, appreciation is experienced when we recognize the value of something outside ourselves. We can appreciate the beauty of a sunset or an artist's work. For this reason, appreciation is a complete departure from the ego-based mind.

Love: Though it may sound cliché, love is the most powerful emotion if it is unconditional love. Most relationships experience conditional love, meaning that we feel love for our partners as long as they meet our expectations.

Conditional love retains the remnants of the ego-based mind and the sense of separation that accompanies it. In conditional love, our sense of separation is temporarily suppressed as long as our partner meets our needs. Our partner will eventually not meet our expectations, and our sense of separation and fear will surface again.

In unconditional love, we have complete acceptance and appreciation for the object of our love, regardless of whether they meet our expectations. This occurs because our love for others has more to do with who they are than it is meeting our needs.

When one experiences unconditional love, we no longer experience a sense of separation or fear of loss, which is why love is the most powerful emotion.

In the next chapter, we will look at how the suppression of emotions lowers our vibrational frequency and invites negative emotions.

Chapter 3:
The Shadow Self

T here is a realm of the human condition of which almost nothing is known. Yet, this realm is all pervasive in every moment of our existence. The realm that I speak of is consciousness. Consciousness is what makes it possible for us to experience the world as well as ourselves. Without consciousness, there can be no experience. Consciousness is the precursor of experience.

We do not know where consciousness is located, its origin, or how it is created. In other words, we know next to nothing about it other than that it exists within us and other living beings. However, there is one thing that we do know, which is that our memories appear and fade within the field of consciousness.

You may have a vivid memory of childhood that you will carry with you for as long as you live. Other memories drift away from the light of our awareness and find themselves dwelling in the depths of our subconscious.

The consciousness and subconscious are not two different things. There is only one consciousness. There is an aspect of ourselves that determines whether our memories will remain in our awareness or be pushed into the abyss of the subconscious.

The aspects of ourselves that we suppress become part of what is known as the shadow self. Even though these aspects are suppressed, that does not mean they do not influence our lives. Our shadow self has a greater influence on us than our conscious self. Let us say that a child has an emotionally unavailable parent. A child learns to trust by how their parent responds to them. A child depends on their parent for all their physical and emotional needs.

If the parent is responsive to the child's needs just some of the time, the child will learn that they cannot depend on their parent to meet their needs. Because of this, the child is unable to trust. The child may associate their parent's lack of responsiveness as a sign of something wrong with them. They may believe they are the source of the problem. This psychological pain can be great, so the child suppresses their thoughts and feelings. In suppressing them, they become part of the shadow self.

Because their thoughts and feelings are surpassed, the child will have no memory of them. Though these suppressed aspects evade the child's awareness, they will continue influencing their decision-making.

As the child grows older, they enter an intimate relationship with a partner. The child wants to become emotionally initiated with their partner, but they fear being hurt. As a result, they back off. They are now torn between the desire for emotional intimacy and fear. Even if their partner does their best to support them, they will continue to be conflicted until they are willing to address their past.

The pattern of negative emotions we experience is the continued expression of our shadow selves. If we have a habit of becoming angry, frustrated, fearful, or any other negative emotion, it is because our shadow aspects are continuing to put forth their energies.

The only way to deal with our shadow aspects is to bring them back into the light of awareness and learn to accept them for what they are. They need to become integrated into our sense of identity. By doing this, these negative emotions will lose their power. Again, emotions are energy. If energy is constrained, its pressure will build. If we let energy flow freely, it will release its pressure and loses its negative influence.

The way to deal with negative emotions is to form a new kind of relationship with them. We need to treat them as part of us that long for expression rather than something we try to dismiss from our lives.

A Healthy Approach to Emotions

As mentioned earlier, we have been raised in a society that has traditionally had an unhealthy view of emotions. Because of this, seeing a mental health professional came with the risk of being stigmatized as weak. Even today, employee health benefits often subordinate mental health care to medical. Fortunately, our society is changing, and progress has been made to promote the importance of emotional health; however, we still have a long way to go.

The topic of emotional health affects everyone, and each one of us can make a difference in the emotional well-being of ourselves and those around us. Our emotional being has a direct effect on those with whom we engage. If we take care of ourselves, we will positively impact the emotional well-being of others. When we feel emotionally balanced, they will sense that. When that happens, they will feel calmer and may even be inspired to create changes in themselves.

In the remaining chapters of this book, we will explore the negative emotions in greater detail. You will learn how they impact you and what you can do to deal with them.

Chapter 4:
Stress: The Trigger of Negative Emotions

I would like to begin with an important point. Stress is not an emotion. Rather stress is how your mind and body respond to a perceived threat. I have devoted this chapter to stress because most of our negative emotions arise from stress. By understanding how stress affects the mind and body, you will gain important knowledge when dealing with negative emotions.

What Is Stress?

Stress is a natural part of life. Although stress is viewed negatively by most, it has beneficial aspects. Stress causes us to challenge ourselves, and it causes us to grow as people. Without stress, there would be no need to challenge ourselves. Stress becomes a problem when we do not know how to manage it.

As stated earlier, stress is how the mind and body respond to a perceived threat. I am repeating this statement because it is significant. The first part of this statement is "stress is how the mind and body respond." You may have heard of the phrase "fight or flight" response. If an animal feels threatened, it will either fight back or flee.

The "fight or flight" response is a mechanism within our bodies that is activated when a threat is perceived. This brings us to the last part of the statement, "... to a perceived threat." This part of the statement means that the "fight or flight" response occurs when we "believe" that there is a threat. In other words, we interpret the situation to be threatening.

I happen to be interested in snakes, and I enjoy working with them when I can. Others are terrified of snakes. Snakes do not cause our bodies to respond with the "fight or flight response." Rather, it is our perception of snakes that makes this happen.

Stress and Body Chemistry

Stress affects the body in profound ways. When we are stressed, our body prepares to fight or take flight. Our heart and breathing rate speed up, as does our reaction time. We become more alert, and the blood supply to certain body parts, such as the digestive system, is reduced. This occurs because these parts of the body are not important during times of threat. The blood is redirected to the parts of the body that need to be engaged, such as the muscles.

These changes in the body occur as a result of how stress affects the body's chemistry. When we perceive a threat, our bodies respond by releasing various hormones that prepare the body for action. When we interpret a situation as threatening, the brain sends messages to different parts of the body to prepare for the situation.

One of those body parts is the adrenal glands. These glands are found near the kidneys. The adrenal glands release the hormones adrenalin and cortisol. These two hormones create the "fight or flight" response in the body. This response leads to an increase in heart rate and blood pressure, muscle contractions, and racing thoughts. These, as well as many other bodily changes, prepare us for dealing with the perceived threat. When the threat is gone, the body's chemistry returns to normal.

The body's stress response is something that we share with the rest of the animals. It is intended to keep us from bodily injury or death. It is meant for our survival. However, we humans have, for the most part, advanced to an existence where the threat of being attacked by a predator is no longer a major concern. We live in a modern society where threats to our survival are almost nonexistent.

Despite this, our "fight or flight" response is still with us. Instead of responding to the threat of predatory animals or warring clans, we face the threats of modern society.

How Stress Shows Up in Our Lives

There are two kinds of stress, acute and chronic. Acute stress is the kind of stress that occurs when we have a job interview, give a speech, or see the dentist. In other words, it is the kind of stress we experience when the perceived threat is temporary. Our bodies return to their normal chemistry when the perceived threat is gone.

The other kind of stress is chronic stress. Chronic stress involves longtime exposure to a potential threat. Examples of these kinds of threats include staying in a job that you hate or in an unhealthy relationship. Other examples include being in a domestic violence situation, a war zone, or experiencing financial hardship.

Chronic stress is different from acute stress. Since the source of stress is long-term, the "fight or flight" response does not end, and the body does not return to normal. Instead, the "fight or flight" response becomes constant. It becomes the new normal. This stress response system that was designed to get you to respond to a threat becomes a threat to your mind and body. The chemical response by the body starts hampering its functioning. Chronic stress can affect the body in the following ways:

The Musculoskeletal System: It is part of the "fight or flight" response for the body's muscles to tighten. The purpose of this is to protect the body. When the threat is gone, the muscles relax. With chronic stress, the muscles stay tight. When this happens, it can lead to migraines and muscle tension.

The Respiratory System: Chronic stress causes rapid breathing and shortness of breath. When this occurs in those who have a respiratory illness, their symptoms can be exacerbated.

The Heart: Chronic stress can lead to elevated blood pressure, hypertension, heart attack, or stroke.

The Endocrine System: Chronic stress has been linked to diabetes, obesity, and immune disorder.

The Gastrointestinal System: There is direct communication between the gastrointestinal and brain systems. Chronic stress can cause problems with the proper functioning of the gastrointestinal system, including stomach pain and bloating. When this occurs, the communication between the gastrointestinal and the brain is impaired. This can result in negative emotions and the inability to think.

The Reproductive System: In males, chronic stress can reduce testosterone production, lower libido, and cause erectile dysfunction. In females, chronic stress can alter menstruation patterns, reduce sexual desire, and make it more difficult for them emotionally during pregnancy and postpartum. Mentally, chronic stress can lead to:

- Difficulty in concentrating
- Difficulty in thinking clearly
- Problems with memory
- Negativity
- Low self-esteem
- Difficulty in making decisions
- Moodiness
- Irritability
- Depression
- Anxiousness
- Feelings of guilt
- Feelings of agitation

The way that stress affects the body and mind needs to be viewed as interconnected with each other. Any negative impact on the body will affect the mind. Similarly, any negative impact on the mind will affect the body. The mind and body are one. Stress is a major cause of negative emotions. For this reason, how we handle our negative emotions will affect our bodies, while the way we treat our bodies will impact our emotions.

Ways to Manage Stress

There are many kinds of stress management methods that you can choose from. The stress management methods in this section include lifestyle changes, mind & body exercises, and therapy.

1. Lifestyle Changes

The stress reduction methods in this section involve basic lifestyle changes:

Aerobic Exercise: Aerobic exercise is an excellent way to reduce stress, and it does so in several ways. To begin with, doing aerobic exercise leads to greater quality sleep. Sleep, particularly deep sleep, has been shown to reduce stress by revitalizing body and brain functions. Additionally, aerobic exercise elevates mood, which it does by releasing endorphins, a hormone that brings about feelings of well-being. This is the same hormone that creates "runner's high." Aerobic exercise includes activities like running, cycling, swimming, or dancing. If your schedule makes it difficult to find the time to exercise, find a way to incorporate aerobic activity into your regular schedule by doing things like:

- Ride your bicycle instead of driving when you are able.
- Use the stairs instead of using the elevator.
- When parking, choose the parking space furthest away from your destination.
- Spend part of your lunch hour taking walks.

A Healthy Diet: Eating healthy is good for your health. However, did you know that a healthy diet can help reduce stress? Eating healthy can strengthen your immune system, elevate your mood, and reduce your blood pressure. Conversely, eating processed and junk food, which contain added fats and sugars, do the opposite. The challenge is that junk food often seems more tempting when we feel stressed.

To eat healthy, choose a diet that consists of lean protein and complex carbohydrates by eating meat, fish, eggs, and nuts. Also, eat foods that

20

contain high levels of antioxidants. Examples of such foods include spinach, strawberries, blueberries, and dark chocolate.

Also, foods that contain Omega-3 fatty acids, magnesium, and Vitamin C help the body deal with stress. Foods that are high in Omega-3 include fish such as salmon, mackerel, herring, and sardines. Omega-3 can also be found in walnuts and soybeans. Foods high in magnesium include dark chocolate, nuts, whole grains, fatty fish, leafy greens, bananas, and avocados. Foods high in Vitamin C include citrus fruits, broccoli, red cabbage, bell peppers, cantaloupe, and kiwi fruit.

Set Yourself Up for Quality Sleep: Sleep difficulties are a common result of stress, which may indicate insomnia. You may have insomnia if you have difficulty falling asleep three times a week for a minimum of three months. Additionally, a lack of sleep can lead to further stress. Developing healthy habits can help you sleep better to break this vicious cycle. These include:

- Maintain a Sleep Schedule: Get between six and eight hours of sleep, which is the recommended amount of sleep for a healthy adult. Additionally, go to bed and wake up each day at the same time. Doing this will help get your body in synch for when it is time to sleep.

- Watch What You Eat and Drink: Do not go to bed either hungry or full. Large meals should be consumed at least two hours before going to bed. Also avoid alcohol, caffeine, or nicotine because they act as stimulants.

- Make Your Bedroom Sleeping Friendly: Do what you can to make your bedroom quiet, cool, and dark. These conditions will make it more conducive for sleep. Also, avoid using your electronic devices as light in the evening can make it more difficult to fall asleep.

- Avoid Daytime Naps: Taking daytime naps can make it more difficult to go to bed at night. If needed, make your naps for less than an hour.

Connecting With Others: Of all the ways to deal with stress, one of the most powerful ways is to spend time with others. Better yet, spend time with people who you can share your feelings with. While you may want to avoid people, your body knows better.

Connecting with others reduces stress (Biggers, 2018). The reason for this has to do with the hormone oxytocin. Oxytocin is a neurotransmitter that is produced by the hypothalamus. It is also the hormone of relationships in that it promotes romantic feelings, bonding, trust, and empathy.

As stated earlier, it is a natural tendency to not feel like socializing when you are feeling stressed. Your stress level is impacted by how you respond to other people. You can feel more comfortable with others by learning to manage your responses.

You can manage your responses by not making any commitments that you feel uncomfortable about, or that you cannot keep. Also, before responding, take a few seconds to think about what you are going to say before saying it. If you feel angry, then walk away until you feel calmer.

2. Mind & Body Exercises

Learning how to gain greater control of your mind and body will allow you to activate the body's relaxation response and reduce stress.

Mindfulness: Fear can only exist when we are anticipating the future. Also, the fear that we experience becomes metabolized by the body. For this reason, people who find themselves caught up in war zones or stress-filled environments age faster than those who are not exposed to such environments.

The power of practicing mindfulness is that it brings our attention back to the present moment. When our attention is on the present moment, fear ceases to exist, stress dissolves, and a sense of calm prevails.

By focusing on the present moment, the volume of the mental noise in our heads is lowered. Thoughts have no power of their own. Instead, their apparent power is derived from the attention that we give them. When our attention is on the present moment, we are giving more attention to what we are experiencing and less to our thoughts.

Another benefit of practicing mindfulness is that it helps regulate negative emotions. Learning to become mindful is all about being aware of what you are experiencing at the moment without judgment. Mindfulness is about having complete acceptance of whatever enters our awareness.

Rather than suppressing negative thoughts or getting caught up in them, being mindful allows for observing them. To observe a negative thought means to be aware of it. This also applies to negative emotions. When you cease to get involved with your negative emotions and observe them instead, they will lose their potency.

One of the easiest ways to practice mindfulness is to place your attention on your breathing. Focus your attention on what you are experiencing as you breathe in and out. By focusing on the sensations of breathing, you will remain in the present moment. The following is a simple mindfulness exercise that you can use:

Basic Meditation: This meditation exercise involves focusing on your breath. Doing so will remove your attention from your thoughts, which will lead to relaxation.

1. Get in a comfortable position, close your eyes, and relax.

2. Breathe naturally. Pay attention to the flow of your breath.

3. As you breathe, focus on the sensations you experience as you inhale and exhale. If it is easier for you, pay attention to the rising and falling of your abdomen.

4. When you find yourself distracted by thoughts, return your attention to the sensations of your breath. Have complete acceptance of whatever you experience and do so without judgment.

5. By practicing this meditation, you will be able to calm your mind.

Deep Breathing Techniques: We live in a stressful world, which affects us in ways we may be unaware of. One of those ways is our breath. Most of us have developed bad breathing habits that we do not breathe properly. Our breaths are shallow rather than deep. When we do not breathe properly, our stress is compounded. The breath is a natural stress reliever, but only if we breathe properly.

As stated earlier, the body goes into the "fight or flight" mode when we perceive a threatening situation. When this happens, stress hormones flood the body to put it in a position of high alert.

When the threat ends, the body returns to its normal state. What allows the body to return to its normal state is the parasympathetic nervous system (PNS). PNS is part of the "fight or flight" mechanism that returns the body's physiology to normal. Deep breathing is an effective way of activating the PNS. The following are breathing exercises that you can do to breathe more deeply.

- Basic Diaphragm Breathing: When doing this breathing technique, it is recommended that you perform it while lying down.
    1. Get into a lying down position, making sure that you are comfortable.
    2. Let your shoulders relax so that they sink downward.
    3. Place one hand on your chest and the other on your abdomen.
    4. Inhale through your nose. Do so naturally; do not force it.
    5. Notice your breath as it travels from your nostrils to your abdomen.
    6. Focus on your abdomen as it rises while keeping your chest as still as possible.
    7. Pull your lips inward like you were drinking through a straw, then exhale slowly. Try to keep your exhalation for four seconds.

8. As you exhale, notice your abdomen contracting.

9. Repeat these steps several times.

- 4-7-8 Breathing: This breathing technique is a lot different from normal breathing. For this reason, it takes time to get used to it. When first starting, practice at least twice a day but only do four cycles of this technique per session. As you get used to this technique, you can increase the number of cycles per session. Also, when first practicing this technique, you may feel lightheaded. This feeling will pass as you get more used to it.

    1. Start by sitting straight in a comfortable position.

    2. Place your tongue to press against the back of your upper teeth and hold it there.

    3. Exhale from your mouth and let the airflow around your tongue, creating a whooshing sound. It may be helpful if you can draw your lips inward when doing this.

    4. With your mouth closed, inhale through your nose for a count of four.

    5. Hold your breath for a count of seven.

    6. Exhale through your mouth for a count of eight. When exhaling, make a whooshing sound.

    7. Steps 1-6 count form one cycle. Repeat this exercise for three additional cycles.

Biofeedback: By using feedback, you can learn to consciously control various body functions, including heart rate, muscle tension, and blood pressure. When you have learned to do so, you can then manage these functions when experiencing stress.

Biofeedback provides you with information about your body through sensors that are placed on key parts of your body. As you get feedback from the various body functions, you learn what you need to do to duplicate those results in the future. In other words, biofeedback allows you to read how your body is performing at any given moment. When you learn to read your body, you can gain control of its functioning.

3. Therapy

Seeing a therapist can be very helpful in reducing stress as they can help you identify the causes of your stress and learn coping skills and ways to manage stress. The following therapies have proven effective in reducing stress:

Cognitive Behavioral Therapy (CBT): CBT is growing in popularity as a therapy because it is effective in treating a wide spectrum of psychological conditions, including:

- Anxiety disorders
- Depression
- Substance abuse
- Marital problems
- Eating disorders
- Severe mental illness

Reasons for CBT's popularity include the fact that there is plenty of scientific evidence to support its effectiveness in creating change in thinking and behavior. CBT is more effective than most other therapies or medications (Otte, 2011).

CBT differs from other kinds of psychological therapies in its guiding principles:

- Our psychological challenges are based on disempowering thinking.
- Our psychological challenges are based on patterns of disempowering thinking that we learned.
- We can learn more empowering ways of coping with our challenges, which will lead to the reduction of symptoms and living our lives more effectively.

During CBT sessions, you will learn to identify any limiting thinking that you may have and replace it with more empowering ones. You will also better understand your motivations while learning problem-solving skills.

Psychodynamic Therapy: As with CBT, psychodynamic therapy will help you identify patterns of thinking that lead to certain behaviors. However, this kind of therapy is best for long-term issues that you may be dealing with where other mental health conditions, such as depression and anxiety, are involved.

Behavioral Therapy: As with CBT, behavioral therapy is also directed toward changing behavior. Unlike CBT, it focuses on behaviors rather than thought patterns. This therapy is based on the idea that the behaviors we demonstrate today originated from previous behaviors. Based on this philosophy, you can learn to change your behavioral responses to stress to avoid feeling stressed in the future. This therapy works best for phobias, anxiety, and attention-deficit hyperactivity disorder (ADHD).

Exposure Therapy: Traditionally used to treat phobias and anxiety disorders, exposure therapy is often used to help clients out with issues of avoidance of certain situations, people, places, or objects. Exposure therapy can be helpful with chronic stress if one avoids certain situations to avoid feeling stressed.

Exposure therapy involves working with a therapist to gradually expose a person to those things that trigger them, thus causing them to avoid them. By doing this, the person will gradually become accustomed to the situation, hence lowering their stress.

Group Therapy: With certain stressful events, group therapy can be helpful. Examples of such events include the loss of a child, divorce, or a natural disaster. A trained therapist facilitates group sessions. The benefits of this kind of therapy are that you will feel more empowered and realize that you are not alone in what you are going through.

In the next chapter, we will explore the emotion that is often associated with stress, which is depression.

Chapter 5:
The Emotion of Depression

D epression is a mood disorder that leads to persistent feelings of emptiness, sadness, and the loss of joy and pleasure. Depression is a separate condition from other moods, such as grief. It can last anywhere from a few weeks to years. In many cases, depression can be chronic, where there are periods of improved mood and then relapses.

Left untreated, depression can negatively impact relationships, work, and maintaining good health. When severe, it can lead to suicide. Worldwide, depression is considered to be the leading cause of disability, meaning that it interrupts daily functioning (WHO, 2023).

What follows is information regarding the symptoms, depression types, and ways to cope with depression.

Depression Symptoms

Symptoms commonly associated with depression include:

- Continuous depressed mood
- The loss of interest in once pleasurable activities
- Changes in body weight and eating habits
- Slowness of movement
- Being agitated
- Sleeping difficulties or sleeping most of the time
- Fatigue or low energy
- Strong feelings of worthlessness or guilt
- Difficulty in making decisions or concentrating
- Suicidal thoughts or attempts to commit suicide
- Chronic pain

- Headaches
- Digestive issues

If an individual demonstrates five of these symptoms within two weeks, they may have depression (NLM).

Forms of Depression

The following are common forms of depression. In describing them, their symptoms have been omitted as they are similar and were previously mentioned. Common forms of depression include the following:

Major Depressive Disorder (MDD): Feeling sad or depressed is normal when we are experiencing a difficult time in our lives. Losing a relationship or a job can bring about signs of depression. However, MDD, also known as clinical depression, is characterized by the person being persistently depressed and showing a lack of interest in activities they used to enjoy. These symptoms need to occur for at least two weeks before major depressive disorder can be diagnosed (NLM).

MDD is classified as a chronic condition; however, it presents itself in episodes that can last weeks or even months (NLM). MDD is often associated with mental health conditions, including panic, social anxiety, substance abuse, and obsessive-compulsive disorders.

Persistent Depressive Disorder (PDD): Also known as dysthymia, is a depressive disorder that is long-term and continuous. Also, the symptoms are the same as other depressive disorders. Persistent depressive disorder differs from MDD in that the symptoms can range from mild to severe.

MDD and PDD have similar symptoms. The main difference is the duration of the symptoms, which health professionals use to diagnose. To diagnose PDD, health professionals look at the symptoms, which need to last for at least two years (Patel and Rose, 2022). With MDD, the expression of symptoms must have at least a two-month gap between them.

Seasonal Affective Disorder (SAD): A form of depression that occurs in the winter months when there is a reduction in daylight. It normally occurs in parts of the country that experience prolonged or severe winters. Treatments for SAD include counseling, light therapy, and medication.

As you can see, the different forms of depression closely resemble each other as they often share the same symptoms. For this reason, it is best to see a health professional if you suspect that you have depression. A health professional can make an accurate diagnosis. Given this, the following are ways that you can cope with depression.

Ways to Cope With Depression

If you have depression, you can regain control of your life by making changes in your lifestyle. The following are suggestions:

Challenge Your Negative Thinking: We all have certain negative beliefs about ourselves, some of which we may not even be aware of. When a person is depressed, they often spend more time focusing on their negative beliefs than they normally do. Additionally, their negative thinking may attract other negative thoughts, which only makes things worse for them.

Whenever you experience a negative thought about yourself, challenge it. Ask yourself if there is any evidence to support it. For example, you may have the belief that you can never do anything right. You can challenge it by thinking about the times you successfully completed a task. Question yourself whenever you use words such as "never" or "always" when thinking about yourself.

Improve Your Self-Image: Depression often is accompanied by feelings of low self-esteem. In turn, low self-esteem often fuels depression. For this reason, it is important to develop your self-image. You can do this by replacing any negative thinking with more positive thoughts.

Just as important as positive thinking, creating a healthy lifestyle is also important. Make lifestyle changes where you eat healthier, exercise regularly, and spend time with family and friends.

Keep a Journal: Journal writing is a helpful way to manage depression because it helps reduce stress. The reason for this is that writing will help you gain clarity in your thinking and in what you are feeling. When writing in your journal, be honest with yourself. Writing daily, even if it is for just a few minutes, can make you feel more relaxed as you will have given a voice to your stress, and depression is often stress-related.

Maintain a Schedule: Keeping up with your routines can have a positive effect on depression. When people become depressed, they often lose their motivation to do anything. The problem is that when they stop following their routines, they feel unproductive, which further affects their self-esteem.

Keep up your routines by maintaining a daily schedule of activities that you need or want to do. By keeping up with your routines you will feel more balanced in your life.

Stay Connected: When feeling depressed, it is normal to want to withdraw from others. However, socializing with others is an important aspect of mental health. Socializing with others can help you from feeling isolated or going into deeper depression.

Though you may not feel like it, spend time with others, even if it is just a walk in the park, going to see a movie, or talking to them on the phone.

Reach Out to Others: Do not hold back from reaching out to family or friends. When you reach out to others, they can inspire or get you motivated to do the things that you need to do to take care of yourself. Being able to express your feelings to others will make you feel less alone, and their feedback can motivate you to do the things that you need to do to feel better about yourself.

Get Plenty of Sleep: When depressed, it is common to have trouble sleeping. However, getting a good night's sleep is important for managing depression. On the other hand, some people spend too much time sleeping when they are depressed.

You can improve your quality of sleep by exercising regularly, avoiding caffeine and nicotine, and keeping a healthy sleeping schedule. Try to get between six and eight hours of sleep, and create a sleep schedule where you go to sleep and wake up at the same time each day.

Exercise Regularly: Besides providing physical benefits, exercise also benefits us emotionally. Regular exercise reduces stress and improves the quality of sleep. Furthermore, exercise releases dopamine, which will make you feel better. If you exercise outdoors that will be an added benefit. Being outdoors will expose you to the sun, which is also important for improving your mood.

Watch Your Diet: Proper nutrition is an important part of managing depression. Foods that are rich in omega-3 fatty acids improve mood. Foods that are rich in omega-3 fatty acids include fatty fish, such as salmon. You can also purchase fish oil supplements. By eating healthier, you will feel healthier, which can improve your self-esteem. In turn, improved self-esteem helps relieve depression.

Avoid Alcohol: Many people turn to alcohol in their attempts to escape the way they are feeling. However, alcohol only makes depression and its symptoms worse. Instead of turning to alcohol, adopt a healthier lifestyle. It is a much more effective way to manage depression.

Speak to a Therapist: While there are a variety of things you can do to cope with depression, it is not recommended that you do them to the exclusion of speaking to a therapist. It is not advisable that you try to overcome depression on your own. By talking to a therapist, you can learn how to make adjustments to cope with stressors and minimize stress.

While depression may make you feel down, there is a negative emotion that will put you on high alert. Fear is the topic of the next chapter.

Chapter 6:
The Emotion of Fear

F ear is an emotion that is universal in that it is experienced by all. This emotion arises when a situation poses a threat to us, either physically, psychologically, or emotionally. The threat can be real or imagined.

Though fear is widely considered to be a negative emotion, it serves an important role in that it puts us on high alert when faced with danger. When we can cope with fear, it will lessen. When we are unable to do so, it will intensify. It is possible to develop a fear of anything; however, certain triggers commonly elicit a fearful response. Common fears include being in the dark, heights, snakes, being rejected, and death.

The reaction to fear has two components to it, biochemical and emotional. The biochemical reaction to fear is a survival mechanism. When faced with a threat, our bodies spring into action. There is an increase in heart rate and adrenaline levels, which puts us on high alert. This reaction is often called the "fight or flight" response.

The emotional response component is very individualized in that fear involves some of the same chemical reactions shared by other emotions, including positive ones. Some people enjoy getting scared, and they may watch horror movies or ride roller coasters to satisfy this desire. Others get involved in extreme sports to experience the adrenaline rush. Others avoid experiencing the emotion of fear whenever they can. Although the physical response to fear is shared by all of us, the emotional response is different for each person.

The Faces of Fear

Fear can appear in different forms, including anxiety and phobias. These emotional responses present themselves differently from fear, but fear forms their foundation.

Anxiety: Anxiety is an unpleasant sense of apprehension of which we may not understand its source. While fear is an emotional response to a definite or known threat, the source of our anxiety may be unclear or unknown to us. Additionally, anxiety is often accompanied by physical symptoms, such as:

- Chest pain
- Rapid heart rate
- Hot flushes or cold chills
- Feeling disconnected or out of control
- Feeling faint or dizzy
- Sweating excessively
- Headaches
- Muscle tension or pain
- Tingling or numbness
- Pulsing or ringing in the ears
- Shortness of breath
- Difficulty breathing
- Tightness in the body
- Nausea or upset stomach

Anxiety and fear are interrelated. Anxiety can lead to fear, and fear can lead to anxiety.

Phobias: While everyone experiences anxiety at one time or another, some experience anxiety regularly, which may mean that they have an anxiety disorder. Those with an anxiety disorder develop a fear of their state of fear. They will do anything to avoid experiencing this emotion in the future and will go out of their way to avoid it. This kind of behavior is what constitutes a phobia.

A phobia distorts the normal fear response by attributing fear to something that presents no danger. Also, you can tell the difference between a fear and a phobia by how they affect you. Having a fear of snakes will not disrupt your life or affect your ability to function in it. You can still enjoy your life. If you have a phobia, it will prevent you from functioning in your life, thus lessening its quality.

Take Charge of Your Fear Response

Most people let their fear response take charge of them, but it does not have to be this way. Instead, you can learn to take charge of your fear response (Robbins). In doing so, you will make fear work for you. The following are suggestions for doing so:

Recognizing What Your Fears Are: As with any challenge, the first step you need to take to overcome your fears is to identify them. Find a time when you can spend a few minutes to become quiet. Take this time to get in touch with what you think and feel. Pay attention to any bodily sensations that you are experiencing.

Next, write down whatever comes to you. When doing this, be specific as you can. As you become more centered, you will realize what your fears are, and you will feel more capable of confronting them. This process can be more effective if you practice mindfulness daily.

See Fear in a Different Light: As stated earlier in this book, emotions are energies that naturally occur within us. Furthermore, these energies serve as messengers. They are how the mind, body, and soul deliver messages to us. Our job is to listen to these messages rather than fearing or avoiding them. The fears or anxieties you may be experiencing may be subconscious and need your attention.

You can discover what they are trying to tell you by moving toward them rather than treating them as something to fear. When you learn what the message of your fear or anxiety is telling you, you can use it to your advantage, and it will no longer run your life. When this occurs, fear becomes an ally.

Reflect on Your Fear: When it comes to fear, we tend to approach it in several ways. We try not to think about it, or we allow ourselves to become engulfed in it. Neither of these approaches serves us. Trying not to think about what you are afraid of only causes its energies to fester and show up in other ways, such as ailments of the mind or body. On the other hand, getting caught up in your fears will leave you with a sense of helplessness.

Instead, try reflecting on your fear by spending time with it. The next time that you experience fear do not try to do anything. Instead, get curious and get to know it. Ask yourself questions like:

- What is behind this fear? What is causing it?
- Am I feeling fear or uncertainty?
- Is what I am experiencing a fear of failure?

By spending time with your fear, you have taken a major step in overcoming it.

Set Goals That Drive You: A common reason we may have difficulty overcoming our fear is the quality of goals we have set for ourselves. Goals that seem elusive or uninspiring can hold us back in fear mode. By changing the quality of your goals, you can develop the drive to move forward with your life. To come up with quality goals, ask yourself questions such as:

1. When I think about the life I desire, what do I see? What does that look like?

2. Knowing what that life looks like, what can I do now to work toward it?

3. Is achieving what I want attainable, and am I willing to commit to it? Is it compelling to me?

4. If I accomplish this goal, will it be fulfilling for me?

If you find yourself feeling driven to achieve this goal, delve deeper into it by asking yourself what your outcome will be if you achieve your goal. When you have identified your outcome, imagine what your life would be like without it and what your life would be like if it became your reality. When you feel a sense of urgency in achieving your goal, you will become inspired to take action. Taking determined action is a powerful way to break through fear.

36

Identify Your Excuses: Fear causes us to procrastinate and not take the action needed to achieve our desired results. When we doubt our ability to achieve our goals, we lie to ourselves by telling ourselves things like "I am too busy," "I am too tired," or "It was a dumb idea."

Making excuses is much simpler than risking failure or putting in the hard work to make your dreams happen.

Again, taking action toward meaningful goals is a great way to move beyond fear. If you find yourself making excuses for not pursuing your goals, challenge them! If your excuse is that you are too tired, do what you need to do to get more sleep. If your excuse is that you do not have enough time, determine what your priorities are and find a way to make time.

Hang Out With the Right Crowd: The old saying "birds of a feather flock together" has a lot of truth to it. Our lives are shaped by the people whom we surround ourselves with. If you want to change your life and reach for your dreams, you would be wise to surround yourself with people with the same mindset. When you surround yourself with people of the same mindset, they will inspire you to achieve your goals and push you to succeed. Also, surrounding yourself with like-minded people will cause you to raise your standards for yourself and make you feel accountable for your actions.

Cultivate a Growth Mindset: When fearful, we tend to stay put. We may be afraid of making mistakes or failing. These fears hold you back by leading you to believe you cannot advance your life. A powerful way to break through your fears is to cultivate a growth mindset.

Developing a growth mindset involves continuing to pursue your dreams while learning to accept the uncertainty you encounter. A growth mindset is one where there is an understanding that overcoming fear will involve facing many challenges along the way but a determination to move forward with one's life. When there is an acceptance that this is the way of the path, you will come closer to achieving your goals.

The Wisdom of Pain: It is our natural inclination to avoid experiencing pain. However, pain, as with all emotions, is a message that contains important information. In this sense, pain can be a teacher. By learning to accept that life is marked by painful moments, those moments become growth opportunities.

Pain is seen less as a threat to your existence and more as a tool for moving forward. Learn to take control of your life by not allowing your past to determine your decisions for the future. Instead, learn from the pain of your past and use it to take charge of your life.

See Tomorrow's Achievements Today: Overcoming fear requires learning how to overcome problems. It is important to identify the problems that you are facing. Once identified, it would be wise to stop focusing on them. Instead, focus on solving them. When you focus on the solution instead of the problem, it will lead you to take action. The key to creating the life that you desire is to give your energy and focus to your goals; the goals that will allow you to achieve your outcome.

Visualization is a way to apply that energy and focus. Make it a daily practice to visualize yourself achieving your goal. Imagine that your goals have already been achieved and are your current reality. When you visualize the achievement of your goal, you are conditioning your brain to believe that your goal's achievement is possible. You will overcome your fear when you believe achieving your goal is possible.

Treat Failure as a Given: One of the predominant fears that most people have is the fear of failure; the failure to achieve their desires. Failure is inevitable in life; however, this does not have to be seen as a negative. The truth is that failure can provide invaluable information that success cannot. By learning to accept failure, you can learn important lessons you can apply in the future.

Everyone fails in life. By learning to accept failure, you will lose your fear of it. When you lose your fear of failure, you will take the needed action to achieve your dreams. Learn to accept failure and move forward with your dreams.

Cognitive Behavioral Therapy (CBT): CBT can be useful for working through negative or distorted thinking that may be causing your fears. A therapist can help you challenge your current thinking, develop more realistic thinking, and learn coping skills. In doing so, you can learn to better understand the source of your fears and more empowering ways to respond to them.

Desensitize Yourself: There is another way to take charge of your fear, which is to overcome it through familiarity. That is achieved by repeated exposure to the source of one's fears. Each exposure involves the person becoming more familiar with the source of their fear. The process of doing so is referred to as systematic desensitization.

Let us say that I am afraid of snakes. The first step I would take is to look at pictures of snakes. While I am doing this, I would monitor myself for the level of fear that I am experiencing. I would keep looking at the pictures until the level of my fear was manageable.

I would then go to a pet shop that sells snakes. I would look at the live snakes until my level of fear became manageable. When I reach that point, I would then touch a captive snake; when I become familiar with that, I would hold the snake.

By becoming more familiar with snakes, my fear of them will vanish. This same technique can be used for any other fears, whether riding in an elevator, flying in a plane, or public speaking. The idea is to take baby steps in facing your fear, with each step bringing you closer to conquering your fears.

Coping Versus Overcoming

There are situations when learning how to cope with one's fears is more practical than overcoming them. I may want to overcome my fear of snakes, but it may be more difficult to overcome my fears that come from my financial struggles. In situations like this, it may be better to learn how to cope with fears. You can do this by doing the following:

Establishing a Social Support System: Find people in your life who support you and can help you work out your feelings.

Mindfulness: Learning to practice mindfulness is an excellent way to learn how to manage your negative thoughts and make you feel more centered.

Stress Management Techniques: There are numerous ways to manage stress, which will help alleviate fear. These include meditation, deep breathing, visualizations, and aerobic exercise.

Live More Healthfully: When you reduce your stress levels, your fears will also lessen. You can reduce your stress by eating healthily, getting plenty of sleep, and exercising.

The emotion of fear comes about when we experience something as being a threat to us. But what happens if the target of the negative emotion is ourselves? This is the topic of the next chapter, which is the emotion of shame.

Chapter 7:
The Emotion of Shame

S hame is the emotion we experience when we go against the social norms we abide by. This emotion can lead to feeling humiliated or embarrassed. When you experience shame continuously, it can lead to the feeling that you are fundamentally flawed.

As with all emotions, shame is a beneficial aspect, which is often not recognized. The experience of shame is intended to get us to behave consistently with our beliefs about what is acceptable behavior.

Shame may have evolutionary significance in that it may have helped us survive as a species. From the earliest part of our history, we needed to follow the cultural norms for the group's survival. Shame may have kept our ancestors on target with the cultural ways at the time (Kammerer, 2019).

However, shame can cause suffering for us when we allow ourselves to internalize this emotion and use it to evaluate our worth rather than evaluate our behavior. Shame should never be confused with self-worth. The emotion of shame can be difficult for some to recognize. However, some signs are associated with shame:

- You are worried or sensitive about how others see you.

- You have feelings of inadequacy or that you have little to offer.

- You are concerned that others may see you as not good enough.

- You fear being your authentic self or sharing your thoughts and feelings.

- You are more concerned about failure when doing something rather than whether it is the right thing to do.

- You have a habit of pushing people away and withdrawing or wanting to be inconspicuous.

In terms of behavior, signs of shame include:

- You look downward rather than eye to eye when you are engaging with others.
- You keep your head low, slump your shoulders, and not stand straight.
- You feel frozen and not able to behave spontaneously.
- You speak very softly or stutter.

How Shame and Guilt Differ

Shame and guilt are often confused with one another; however, they are separate emotions. Shame is an emotion we may attribute to our character or who we are as people. It is the way that we perceive ourselves as not being good enough. Guilt is an emotion that we attribute to a behavior, something we have done that we later regret.

If taken from a healthier perspective, shame and guilt are messages that point to how we can improve as people. Shame is the message that we need to honor other people's boundaries and treat them respectfully. Further, we need to establish boundaries for how we want to be treated. The message of guilt is learning to forgive others and ourselves and improve our conduct.

Types of Shame

There are many forms of shame; however, they fall into four broader categories (Dodgson, 2018). They are as follows:

Unrequited Love: This kind of love is experienced when you love someone, but your love is not reciprocated. This is a form of shame. This kind of shame may be a natural aspect of our development.

There has been research where mothers are instructed to interact with their babies by talking to them while smiling (Clarke, 2022). Later, the mothers were instructed not to react to their babies. Instead, they were told to just stare at them without any emotion. In response, the babies would attempt to gain their mother's attention, but then they would give up and start to cry.

The researchers believed that the mother's lack of empathy resulted in the babies feeling an emotion that is similar to shame. The researchers further suggest that this kind of dynamic may be what is seen when mothers are unable to mirror their child's emotions due to depression or from being overwhelmed with life (Clarke, 2022). This is the kind of parental behavior that leads to attachment disorders.

Unwanted Exposure: Unwanted exposure is what most people think of when they think about shame. This kind of shame occurs when a mistake you made is made public, or you are getting undressed, and someone walks into the room.

Disappointed Expectations: This shame occurs when you fall short of reaching an important goal you set for yourself. Examples of this include not getting the promotion you strived for, or when the relationship that you are in does not work out.

Exclusion: This form of shame comes from not feeling that you fit in. Whether at work, in a group, or a relationship, we all want to feel like we belong, that we are accepted. When something that we do threatens that, we may experience shame.

Responses to Shameful Behavior

In his book, *Guilt, Shame, and Anxiety,* psychiatrist Peter Breggin (Cunic, 2023) identified four kinds of responses that are exhibited when we experience shame:

The Hot Response: The hot response involves deflection from oneself by attacking or lashing out at others to deflect attention from oneself. This behavior is often done impulsively.

Behaviors to Cope With or Conceal Shame: The behaviors for this category involve trying to make oneself inconspicuous by avoiding the attention of others and not disclosing one's thoughts or feelings.

Safety Behaviors to Avoid Shame or Being Discovered: This is the style of those who avoid conflict by behaving emotionally, such as crying or apologizing.

Behaviors to Repair Shame: Those in this category behave in ways that soothe themselves, or they may apologize. An example is that you may have forgotten it was someone's birthday. Your response may be that you tell yourself that you have been very busy, or you do things to show the other person that you are sorry.

Toxic Shame Versus Healthy Shame

We just covered the different types of shame and how we behave when feeling shame. While these classifications may help you identify how you experience shame, it is more important to know the difference between toxic shame and healthy shame.

Toxic shame occurs when we internalize the shame and develop the belief we are inherently flawed inside and that we are inferior to others. When this occurs, the emotion of shame becomes our sense of identity. Those who experience toxic shame may try to appear perfect to others to distract themselves from how they feel inside.

Healthy shame results in creating a sense of humility and reminds you of the importance of boundaries. It reminds you to respect the boundaries of others and the boundaries you need for yourself. Additionally, shame teaches us how our behavior affects others. When shame teaches us how to better relate to others and ourselves, this emotion has done its job.

When we do not healthily deal with shame, it can hurt how we feel about ourselves and our behavior. Shame can lead to:

- Believing that something is wrong with you and that you are flawed

- Withdrawing socially

- Addictions

- People pleasing

- Perfectionism or overachieving behaviors

- Becoming defensive and responding by bullying or shaming others

- An inflated ego conceals your lack of self-worth, which is what is termed a narcissistic personality

- Physical health issues

- Feeling sad or depressed

- Feeling lonely or empty

- Low self-esteem

- Difficulty trusting others

- A reluctance to reach out to others or seek therapy

- Compulsive behaviors

Any of these behaviors will have a negative impact and compound the existing problems from feeling shame.

Dealing With Shame

If you are dealing with shame, there are things you can do to heal it. However, to do this requires you to face your shame and be willing to engage with it. There are three steps to this process, explore, embrace, and accept.

Explore: The first step is to get to know your shame by exploring it. Unless you can identify the cause of your shame, you cannot heal it. You can explore your shame by finding out where it came from and how it has influenced your life. To do this, pay attention to the emotions you experience as you encounter different situations.

Identify the situations that cause the emotion of shame to be triggered. When you feel triggered, how does it make you feel? When you think about the times that you were shamed in the past, did you learn anything from the experience? How does shame affect your life today? By asking these and other questions, you will be able to get greater clarity of why you feel the way you do. Doing this exercise will bring the light of awareness to the area of your life that has been kept in the dark.

Embrace Your Shame: Having explored your shame, the next step is to embrace it. Doing this may seem unusual, but you must take this step. Remember, our emotions are forms of energy. If you suppress energy, it will build and create greater pressure. What we resist will persist. If you embrace any emotion, you are allowing its energies to be released.

This step of the exercise requires you to learn to love and accept yourself. To do this, you must have support from others who will treat you accordingly. Think of people in your life who you can trust to support you in this manner. If you cannot find people like this, you can join a support group. The idea is to treat yourself with unconditional love and be with others who will show you the same. You can practice unconditional love by doing the following:

- Remind yourself to love yourself unconditionally whenever you experience shame.

- Demand from yourself that you will be honest with others and yourself.

- When you experience shame, do not avoid the feeling. Instead, talk about how you are feeling.

- Honor the suffering you experience by not making excuses for it or diminishing it. Give your suffering its legitimacy. By doing this, you will gain a greater perspective on your shame. If, for any reason, you have difficulty with these steps, please consider speaking to a therapist.

Acceptance: As you go through the exploration and embracing stages of this process, you will begin to identify your beliefs about yourself. Some of those beliefs will be disempowering. In this step, it is time to abandon the disempowering beliefs and start accepting and loving yourself for who you are.

Accept that making mistakes is okay; it does not make you less. If there is someone you know who has a healthy sense of self, see if they would be willing to be a mentor for you. Choose someone who will hold you accountable for making healthy decisions that lead to honoring yourself. Again, if you do not have someone like this, consider finding a therapist who can take on that role for you.

Are You Being Shamed by Someone Else?

As indicated earlier, it is important to surround yourself with people who accept and support you in moving beyond your shame. But what if someone in your life is intentionally shaming you? Is there someone in your life who is like that? The following are the signs to look out for:

- They are loud when they speak to you.

- They are confrontational when addressing you.

- You feel like they are condescending to you.

- They try to stare you down, or they do not offer any eye contact.

- They are mocking or belittling in their comments to you.

- They put you down in front of others.

- They are aggressive in their stance or body language.

If someone is shaming you, realize that their behavior is inappropriate. Do not internalize the shame or let it affect you. Instead, be assertive and insist that they treat you with respect. There are many resources available for learning how to be assertive.

How to Handle Long-Term Shame

If you have been carrying shame for a prolonged period, it may be difficult for you to apply the suggestions offered in this chapter. It is important to understand that there is a lot of complexity to shame, which can make it difficult to overcome it on your own.

Anyone can overcome shame if they are willing to put in the work and learn to embrace and accept this emotion. Seek help from a mental health professional so that they can guide you through the process.

Remember, you are worth it. You are not your shame. Rather, you have allowed shame to define you. You can learn to define yourself in an empowering and loving way that allows you to express the truth of who you are.

In the next chapter, we explore the emotion of grief.

Chapter 8:
The Emotion of Grief

G rief is the emotion of loss. Because grief represents the loss of someone or something that we love or is important to us, the effects of grief on us can feel all-encompassing. As an emotion, grief has great variability as how it is expressed can differ with each person. Additionally, the emotion of grief can also be accompanied by feelings of confusion and guilt, which makes things more complicated for the grieving person.

Moreover, grief is deeply personal. Because of this, there are no timelines of when someone should stop grieving. For some, the experience of grief may be only short-term. Others may experience it for years. What is important is that this emotion be expressed. Trying to deny or suppress grief will only prolong the time needed to recover from it.

Many do not understand that grief can be experienced from losses beyond a partner, parent, or friend. People may experience grief due to the following:

- Divorce
- Changing a life's role
- Death of a pet
- Loss of a job
- Loss of a home
- Loss of possessions

Because we often do not associate grief with these kinds of losses, those who are grieving may not feel acknowledged for what they are experiencing. Regardless of the reason for grieving, the process of working through grief is the same.

The Stages of Grief

The stages of grief are a natural process for the processing of a loss. This process cannot be controlled or manipulated. There is no right or wrong way to grieve. The process of grief needs to play out according to its own pace. For the one grieving, they need to allow the process to happen. Those who are around the one grieving should support the person as they go through the process.

The following are the stages of grief:

Denial: Denial is the stage when one first learns of the loss. Denial is a defense mechanism that guards against the initial flood of emotions. In denial, you may feel numb or disbelief over what had happened.

Anger: When reality sets in, there is a recognition of the pain being experienced due to loss. The pain may leave you feeling helpless, which then leads to anger. This anger is directed outside oneself and may include other persons, God, or life itself. Anger can also be directed at the one who has passed, with the griever being angry that they left them alone. Regardless of who the target of the anger is, anger is another defense mechanism by masking the pain one feels from their loss.

Bargaining: At this stage, the grieving person starts questioning themselves about what they could have done differently. The person may have thoughts like:

- "If only I had … "
- "What if I had … "

Depression: At this stage, there is a recognition of one's loss and its impact on one's life. This stage is marked by signs of depression that may include:

- Sadness
- Crying
- Difficulty sleeping

- Loss of appetite

- Loneliness

- Regret

- Feeling overwhelmed

Acceptance: This is the stage of the process when one accepts the reality of their loss. Sadness is experienced, but there is also a recognition that one can resume living one's life. It is important to remember that each person experiences grief differently, which is also true with the five stages of grief. Each person will go through these stages in their way.

Some people may bounce back and forth between the stages, while others may skip some of the stages entirely. Also, even when one completes the five stages, one may experience a trigger that causes one to experience grief again. Triggers can include things like the anniversary of their loss or a song.

How to Cope With Grief

The following are coping strategies that you can use when experiencing grief:

Acknowledge Your Grief: Grieving is a natural and necessary process. If you do not allow yourself to grieve, its negative energies will be retained within you, which can affect you both emotionally and physically. The healthiest thing to do is to experience your grief and let its process proceed.

Letter Writing and Journaling: If your loss of a loved one occurred recently, express your feelings toward them by writing a letter to them. Doing this will provide a chance to express yourself, which will help with coping.

Also, keep a journal where you record your thoughts and feelings daily. As part of your journaling, write about your positive memories. This can help in the healing process.

Reach Out to Others: Though it can be difficult, do not give in to the desire to isolate yourself. Talking to others and sharing your feelings is an important part of the healing process.

Remember, Everyone Is Different: Everyone grieves differently; there is no right or wrong way to grieve. Acknowledge that what you are experiencing is your way of grieving.

Do Not Be Surprised: Do not be surprised if your grief resurfaces later on. Birthdays and holidays are just some of the events that can trigger feelings of grief. By learning coping skills, you can better deal with this should it arise.

When to Seek Professional Help: If you or someone you love is going through grief, and they do not seem to be improving, it may be time to seek professional help. Signs that professional help may be needed include:

- Difficulty maintaining your normal routine, such as cleaning your home or going to work
- Not moving beyond the depression stage
- Thoughts of harming themselves
- The inability to move beyond self-blame

Seeing a therapist will help you explore your emotions, learn coping skills, and manage your grief. If depressed, a doctor may be able to prescribe medication to help with your mood.

How You Can Help Others

Given that everyone experiences grief differently, the best way you can support someone in their grieving is to honor what they are going through and be there for them. Avoid judging them or trying to change how they feel. Do not tell them what they should be doing. Instead, offer them practical help and acknowledge their loss.

Also, listen to them without judgment and ask them questions. Doing this will help them process their feelings. Asking questions will also help the other person feel that they are being validated for what they are experiencing.

It is important to recognize that there is no timetable for the grieving process. How long it takes for someone to go through the five stages of grieving can depend on a range of factors, including their age, beliefs, their support network, and how the loss occurred.

When people have difficulty moving through the five stages of grief, they may remain in emotional pain. When this happens, some may try to numb their feelings through alcohol, drugs, or other means that can be harmful. Any of these things can only provide a temporary escape from one's emotional pain.

The only way out of the emotional pain is to go through the five stages, and a therapist can help guide you. The following are suggestions for going through the healing process:

- Be patient with yourself. Accept whatever feelings you are experiencing and realize that they are part of the grieving process.

- Spend time with others. Do not isolate yourself.

- Take good care of yourself. Eat well, exercise, and get plenty of sleep.

- Resume with your interests and do those things that bring you happiness.

- Join a grief support group to share with others who are going through the same thing.

In the next chapter, you will learn about an emotion that happens to be part of the grieving process, which is anger.

A Beacon for Navigating Emotional Storms

"The emotion that can break your heart is sometimes the very one that heals it ..." - Nicholas Sparks

I n life's journey, we often encounter emotional turbulence, navigating through anger, stress, anxiety, and other intrusive feelings. You have likely felt these emotions deeply, perhaps even felt overwhelmed by them, and wondered if anyone else shares your struggle.

The truth is, you are not alone. Many of us grapple with these emotions, seeking solace and strategies to manage them and achieve a sense of inner peace. This shared journey of emotional exploration and healing is what inspired me to pen *Managing Negative Emotions*.

As you immerse yourself in this book, I hope you find comfort in the knowledge that you are part of a larger community, people who, like you, are striving to understand and manage their emotions better. It is a journey that is often challenging, but one that holds the promise of rewarding personal growth.

Now, you have an opportunity to be a beacon of hope for others embarking on this journey. By sharing your honest review of this book on Amazon, you can guide others in their quest for emotional well-being. Your insights into how this book has assisted you, and what they might discover within these pages, can provide invaluable reassurance that they are not alone.

Your voice has the power to illuminate the path for others. Your review can lead them toward the resources they need, simply with the click of a button. You hold the power to change lives by sharing your experience, extending a hand of solidarity to those grappling with their emotions.

I am deeply grateful for your support and contribution. Together, we can foster understanding and compassion, creating a world where managing negative emotions is not a solitary struggle but a shared journey toward inner peace. Thank you for your valuable time and for making a difference.

Scan to leave a review

Chapter 9:
The Emotion of Anger

The emotion of anger has evolutionary significance in that it is linked to our survival. We share a survival mechanism known as the "fight or flight" response with the rest of the animal kingdom. This mechanism is part of our nervous system, particularly the sympathetic nervous system.

When we perceive a threat, the sympathetic nervous system puts us on high alert and changes our body's chemistry. There is the release of hormones like adrenaline, our blood pressure rises, and our muscles tense. These and many other changes occur to deal with the threat, be it fighting back or fleeing.

For the most part, we humans do not have to worry too much about threats to our lives. We do not have to worry about a larger predator or a warring tribe threatening our safety. In today's society, these life-and-death situations have been replaced by the stress created by our jobs, relationships, or other non-life-threatening aspects of our lives.

Even though the threats to our survival have been largely eliminated, our "fight or flight" response remains functioning. This response brings about the emotion of anger, even when the perceived threat may be as harmless as an insult.

The Consequences of Anger

As stated earlier, the sympathetic nervous system puts the body on high alert when a threat is perceived. Some of the changes that occur in the body include the release of hormones, increased blood pressure, and an increase in muscle tension. These changes put the body in the best state to deal with the threat. When the threat is gone, the body's chemistry returns to normal.

While anger is one of our basic emotions, it can cause problems when we do not learn to manage it. If we have problems managing our anger, the sympathetic nervous system keeps getting activated, and the amount of time spent in its normal state becomes less frequent. The prolonged time the body spends in the activated state affects our emotional and physical health. Consequences to our health include:

- High blood pressure
- Weakened immune system
- Destruction of neurons in the brain leading to problems with judgment and short-term memory
- Relationship problems
- Sleeping problems
- Digestive problems
- Depression
- Anxiety

If you have a problem with chronic anger or experience outbursts occasionally, you can learn to identify and manage your anger, thus, experiencing a healthier and happier life.

Personality Traits and Anger Problems

Research (Psychology Today, 2023) has identified traits for those who have problems with managing their anger:

- Having a sense of entitlement which is the belief that your privileges and rights make you superior to others
- Focusing on things that are beyond your control as opposed to focusing on what you can control
- Attempting to regulate your emotions by controlling your environment
- Having an external locus of control which is the belief that one's well-being is controlled by factors outside oneself, such as other people's behavior.
- Not being open to other perspectives or viewpoints
- Having little tolerance for feelings of discomfort

- Having little tolerance for ambiguity
- Tending to blame others
- Having a frail ego

Managing Anger

The key to managing any emotion is to first become aware of it. We get caught up in our emotions when we are unaware of them. By becoming aware of our emotions, we can catch them as they arise and then manage them, so they do not get the best of us. The following are ways you can learn to manage your anger:

Support Groups: Join an anger management support group. You will learn from others experiencing similar challenges and approaches to managing anger.

Therapy: Therapy can help you learn to identify triggers of your anger and how you can take responsibility for them. This is done by learning coping skills and practicing problem-solving.

Breathing Techniques: Breathing techniques are excellent for anger reduction. Refer to Chapter 4 for deep breathing techniques.

Emotional Labeling: Emotional labeling is a very simple but effective way to manage anger, but it takes practice. Occasionally, check in with yourself and identify how you are feeling. The more you do this, the more aware you will become of your emotions.

When you identify your emotions, label them. In other words, tell yourself what emotion you are experiencing. When you are accustomed to doing this, you can spot anger when it arises within you. When you label your anger, you will not get caught up in it.

A Problem-Solving Mindset: Rather than allowing anger to drive you when facing problems, become a problem solver instead. Look for ways to solve the problem to benefit you and all stakeholders.

Sleep: It is hard to control anger if you are not getting adequate sleep. Develop a regular sleep pattern where you go to sleep and wake up at the same time each day. It will do you good and help you manage your anger.

Challenge Your Beliefs: Our beliefs determine what we focus on; however, our beliefs are just interpretations of our experiences. Anger occurs when we believe that we are right and that any other perspective is wrong. Learn to challenge your beliefs by looking for evidence to support them. Also, learn to be open to other perspectives.

Avoid the Catharsis Myth: Do not follow the myth that venting anger will make you feel better. This is true only at the moment. Long term, venting your anger will only reinforce it. Naturally, there are times when it is appropriate to vent your anger. However, times like these should be the exception, not the rule.

Is Your Anger Justified?

It is important to point out that anger can be a healthy emotion if it is justified. When determining whether anger is justified, you need to have some context. Anger is justified when you have been treated unfairly, provoked, or when you have witnessed injustice. In situations such as these, anger is a healthy response if expressed in an assertive manner instead of aggressively.

Anger becomes a problem when it is experienced too intensely or too frequently. It is also a problem when anger is expressed in ways that are not healthy. Unhealthy expression of anger includes:

Aggression: Aggression is an unhealthy anger response, regardless of the form it takes. Aggression toward other people, animals, or objects, or the use of hurtful words is not okay.

Passive Aggression: Passive aggression is when one expresses anger indirectly. Examples of passive aggression include:

- Acting grumpy while denying that anything is bothering you

- Expressing your discontent by failing to follow through or procrastinating on a requested task

- Expressing that you feel unappreciated or are a victim of injustice is a way of not addressing a particular problem directly

- Keeping score by keeping track of unaddressed issues from the past and digging them up when you feel wronged by others

- Giving backhanded compliments

- Giving the silent treatment

- You emotionally distance yourself from others without letting them know why

Repressed Anger: Some people learned that showing anger is a bad thing and that it should be kept to yourself. Signs that you may be repressing anger includes feeling defensive when others tell you that you appear angry, being sarcastic, or being passive-aggressive.

When anger is expressed in an unhealthy manner, we increase our chances of experiencing the consequences of anger, described earlier in this chapter.

Healthy Ways of Expressing Anger

The following are healthy ways to deal with anger:

- Acknowledge that anger is a natural emotion that we all have.

- If you feel anger and you feel that you will not be able to control it, remove yourself from the situation until you can calm down.

- Try identifying the specific reason for your anger.

- When you have identified the cause of your anger, come up with different ways to resolve the situation.

- Engage in physical activity like sports or go for a run.

- Share your feelings with someone whom you trust.

If you are having trouble dealing with your anger, you should see a therapist if you cannot do it alone. It is also important to note that depressive and post-traumatic stress disorders are often associated with outbursts of aggression.

Anger is often born from frustration, which is the topic of the next chapter.

Chapter 10:
The Emotion of Frustration

Frustration is the emotion experienced when your goals or expectations are not met. Someone may have had the goal to lose weight by a certain date or expected that their partner would agree with them on an important decision. When these things do not come to fruition, frustration is experienced.

Frequently, the feeling of frustration does not last long. Situations may change, or we get over this feeling. However, there are situations when the feeling of frustration is enduring. When this occurs, it can lead to consequences for our emotional and physical well-being.

Signs of Frustration

The following are indicators that you may be experiencing frustration:

- Losing your temper
- Feeling angry
- Avoiding those with whom you feel frustrated with
- Feeling like you are on edge or anxious

  Changes to your sleeping or eating habits - sleeping and eating more or less than usual
- Feeling overwhelmed
- Using nicotine, alcohol, or other substances as a way to cope
- Mannerisms such as frowning, sighing, or tapping the feet

How Frustration Affects Us

After experiencing frustration, it is not unusual for other emotions to set in, including stress, anger, and sadness. If you find yourself frequently feeling frustrated, it could lead to the following:

Aggressive Behavior: Frustration can lead to anger, and anger, if not managed, can lead to aggression.

Depression: Long-term frustration can lead to feelings of depression.

Low Self-Esteem: Feeling frustrated can cause you to lose confidence in yourself.

Addictions: To cope with frustration, some may turn to cigarettes, alcohol, or drugs.

Dealing With Frustration

Everyone is different in their tolerance for frustration. Some have a high tolerance for frustration, which means they have successful ways of coping with it. Others have a low tolerance for frustration, so they easily become frustrated.

If you have a low tolerance for frustration, you can learn to use strategies that will allow you to respond to frustration healthily. The following are suggestions for coping with frustration:

Seek Therapy: Speaking to a therapist can help you find out your triggers and how to cope with them more empoweringly.

Raise Your EIQ: We all have heard the term "IQ," which means intelligence quotient. However, did you know that there are different forms of intelligence? Emotional intelligence (EIQ) is the ability to:

- Be aware of the emotions you or others are experiencing now

- Being able to evaluate what emotions you are experiencing

- Being able to manage your emotions if needed

Take a Time Out: If you feel frustrated, take a time out. This will allow you to manage your emotions and express yourself when you feel it is appropriate.

Become More Empathetic: Learn to empathize more with others, including those who tend to frustrate you. Remember that everyone is doing the best they can with what they know.

The Transience of Life: Nothing in this life is permanent; everything comes and goes with time. This is especially true with our emotions. The less you hold on to your emotions, the sooner they will pass.

Distractions: When you are feeling frustrated, find a way to temporarily distract yourself that is healthy and will support you in becoming calmer. This includes exercising, watching a movie, or listening to music.

However, there is a fine line when distracting yourself. The proper way to use distractions is to use them only when you feel like you need to calm down. You would then be able to address the problem. Distracting yourself becomes unhealthy when it becomes a pattern for avoiding the issue.

Practice Mindfulness: Practicing mindfulness will teach you to become nonjudgmental about what you are experiencing, including your emotions. With nonjudgment comes the attitude of acceptance. You will also develop greater awareness and be able to spot emotions before you get caught up in them. For all these reasons, learning to become mindful is a powerful way to deal with frustration or any other emotion.

Learn Relaxation Techniques: By using relaxation techniques, you can end the body's stress response so that it can return to calmness. Learning to do so is important because it will help you maintain better health, and you will be less likely to say or do something that you will regret later on because you were frustrated. Relaxation techniques include meditation, exercise, deep breathing, and spending time with others.

Attitude Change: Most of what we experience as being frustrating results from how we mentally process it. In other words, how we perceive things creates frustration, not the situation itself. Individuals who recognize that they control how they see things are less frustrated than those who believe otherwise. This reality is what separates optimists from pessimists. If you tend to be frustrated, you may have a pessimistic outlook. On the other hand, if you become frustrated infrequently, you probably have an optimistic perspective.

Reevaluate Your Lifestyle: When you live a healthy lifestyle, you can handle frustration more easily. If you are frequently frustrated, part of the problem may have something to do with your lifestyle. If this is true for you, a lifestyle change may help. Living a healthy lifestyle involves:

- Eating healthy

- Exercising regularly

- Getting plenty of sleep

- Developing a social support system by finding people who care and can be trusted

Start Journaling: Make a point to journal each day by writing down your feelings and what you are experiencing. Writing down these things will help you gain clarity and relieve your frustration.

When we are frustrated, we feel tension, and that is why frustration has a higher energy level than sadness, which is the topic of the next chapter.

Chapter 11:
The Emotion of Sadness

The emotion of sadness is experienced when we lose something important to us. Sadness can also be caused by having expectations for the future which do not happen. As a result, we may experience sorrow. For this reason, sadness can be associated with other negative emotions, such as depression or anger. However, there is a difference between these emotions.

How Sadness Differs From Depression

Although sadness can be a symptom of depression, sadness is a separate emotion. You can be sad but not depressed. If someone is sad but not depressed, their sadness will come and go. However, if someone has sadness as a symptom of depression, their sadness will be experienced for long periods. Also, it will be experienced more intensely. Moreover, depression often leads to feeling debilitated, making everyday tasks difficult.

How Sadness Differs From Anger

Anger is the emotion we experience when we feel that there has been an injustice to us or someone else. It is a motivating emotion that may cause us to respond by acting. However, our actions may be impulsive. If I am angry because I perceive that someone is bothering my wife, my anger may cause me to behave in a manner that I will later regret.

Though sadness may seem like a negative emotion, it offers benefits. Unlike anger, which is a motivating emotion, sadness is a more reflective one. Sadness causes us to slow down, which gives us more time to think about a situation.

The Signs of Sadness

Not everyone expresses sadness the same way, however, common signs of sadness include:

- Withdrawing socially
- Moving slowly
- Loss of interest in pleasurable activities
- Down-turned mouth
- Downcast eyes or drooping
- Slanted inner eyebrows
- Posture is slumped over
- Change in heart rate

Additionally, people commonly report feeling the following:

- Lonely
- Distressed
- Depressed
- Anxious
- Grief

The Benefits of Sadness?

Though chronic sadness can hurt you emotionally and physically, short-term sadness does offer benefits (Arias, 2020):

Expand Your Thinking: When in familiar situations, we often get along by using intuition or mental shortcuts. In other words, we are not focusing on the details of the situation. We are running on autopilot. When we feel sad, these automatic tendencies are diminished, and we need to pay more attention. Your sadness may be helping you more accurately process what is happening in a situation so that you will be more successful in the future.

Become a Better Communicator: Research has demonstrated that when sad, we communicate more effectively than when we are in a positive mood. When we are sad, we better understand the ambiguities of a conversation. Further, we are more effective in persuading others.

The research further showed that these improvements in our communication do not happen consciously. Rather they occur automatically. For this reason, the researchers recommend that we talk to others when we are sad rather than withdraw from them.

Connecting With Others: It is believed that one of the important functions of sadness is to draw support from others. We tend to want to support others who are sad. However, we tend to withdraw from others when they are angry.

This inclination to support those who are sad may be instinctual, as studies found that just the facial expressions of a person or their tears were enough to trigger a helping response from the study participants.

Develop Resiliency: Another function of sadness is building resiliency by awakening us to reality. Sometimes we have a false sense of control when we are striving to achieve something. Sadness brings us back to reality by demonstrating to us that there are many things in life that we cannot control. In other words, sadness humbles us.

This coming back to reality occurs more frequently as we get older. An example is a chronic illness. There are situations when one has to surrender their efforts to be cured and instead accept their diagnosis and learn to manage it. In this manner, sadness can get us to accept our losses and advance to our new reality.

The Motivator for Positive Change: Research has shown that sadness can motivate you to take steps toward healthy behavioral changes, such as exercising more or quitting smoking. The researchers believe this occurs because sadness causes us to perceive our lives differently.

The Downside of Sadness

With all of the benefits of sadness, it also presents potential consequences. If sadness becomes too intense, or if it is prolonged, it can have negative effects on your health. If sadness is persistent and other symptoms are present, it may indicate depression. Depression has been associated with other health issues, such as cardiovascular disease and cancer.

Coping With Sadness

The healthy approach to sadness is to first accept how you feel. Do not try to resist it or deny what you are experiencing. One of the reasons why meditation or mindful practices help cope with sadness is that sadness is experienced without judgment. One should strive to be present with one's feelings though they may be uncomfortable.

Another effective way to cope with sadness is to spend time in nature. Research shows that nature has a calming effect. By practicing these simple recommendations, you can minimize the negative effects of sadness while enjoying more of its benefits.

Also, journaling can be helpful. By recording your thoughts and feelings, you will gain greater clarity as to why you are feeling the way you are. Developing clarity is the first step to healing.

If your experience of sadness is chronic, it is advisable that you see a health professional, especially if it is interfering with your life and lasting more than two weeks.

Sadness can be one of the negative emotions that are associated with loneliness, which is the topic of the next chapter.

Chapter 12:
The Emotion of Loneliness

L oneliness is another one of those emotions that is experienced by everyone. Additionally, everyone experiences this emotion differently. A child at school, who has difficulty making friends, will experience loneliness differently than a senior citizen who has lost their partner.

When the word "loneliness" comes to mind, we often think about being alone. However, loneliness is a state of mind. Some people are lonely among other people, and some people are alone but who are not lonely.

How Loneliness and Solitude Differ

Loneliness can be defined as the feeling of being isolated while desiring a connection with others. It is the feeling of abandonment, rejection, or separation. Regardless of the feeling, it is experienced as being involuntary. In other words, we do not consciously choose to be lonely. Also, loneliness can negatively impact us mentally and physically. Solitude differs from loneliness in that it is voluntary. It is a decision that we make because we enjoy spending time by ourselves.

Loneliness Is Situational

Numerous factors create loneliness. Examples of these factors include:

- Moving to a new area
- Divorce
- Death of a significant other
- Being isolated
- Depression
- Low self-esteem

Things like divorce or moving to a new area are situational. These are factors that exist outside us. However, some factors are internal, such as depression and low self-esteem. For depression, loneliness can be a symptom of this disorder, as depression may cause one to withdraw from others. Low self-esteem can lead a person to believe that they do not deserve the attention of others, which can lead to isolation. If this persists, it can lead to chronic loneliness.

Personality traits can also contribute to feeling lonely. While many introverts prefer to be alone, they are also less likely to seek connection with others when they need to, such as when facing difficulties. When this happens, they are likely to feel lonely and isolated.

How Loneliness Affects Us

The following are ways that loneliness can affect you mentally and physically:

- Alcohol and drug abuse
- Altered brain function
- Alzheimer's disease progression
- Antisocial behavior
- Cardiovascular disease and stroke
- Decreased memory and learning
- Depression and suicide
- Increased stress levels

In addition to those, there are other ways loneliness affects us indirectly. Studies have shown that lonely adults are less likely to exercise while more likely to eat a non-nutritious diet. They are also less likely to sleep well. All of these factors can contribute to disrupting the body's ability to regulate itself, leading to premature aging.

Moreover, research shows that people who experience less loneliness are more likely to get married, have a higher income, and be more educated.

Loneliness Is on the Rise

Statistics indicate that loneliness is on the increase, particularly among younger people (Holmes, 2023). The survey, conducted in 2019, reveals that 25 % of those between 18-27 of age reported that they did not have close friends, while 22% reported having no friends.

Researchers believe that social media may be partially to blame, indicating that it is the quality of relationships rather than the number of friends that prevents loneliness. What is important is meaningful face-to-face contact that enhances well-being.

Ways to Deal With Loneliness

You can overcome loneliness if you are willing to make changes in your life. The following are suggestions:

Get Involved: Get involved in activities that you enjoy or in community service. Doing this will open you up to opportunities to meet new people, practice your social skills, and cultivate new relationships.

Focus on the Positive: Lonely people tend to avoid approaching others out of fear of rejection. Instead, focus on the positive. Approach others with the mindset that only the positive can happen. If the person you approach is interested in getting to know you, it could be the beginning of a new relationship. If you get rejected, you can think of it as a learning opportunity to improve your approach for the next time.

Quality Over Quantity: Focus on quality, not quantity. Look for people with whom you share similar values, attitudes, or interests. Meeting and developing relationships are always easier when you share something in common.

Find the Root Cause: Loneliness is not a disease; it is a symptom. Loneliness is a symptom of something larger. You may not know what that is, but you can still do something about it. Start taking the necessary steps to help reduce your loneliness by getting more involved with others and forming new connections.

Overcoming loneliness is a journey, so do not expect things to change overnight. By applying yourself each day, you will feel more confident in your self-worth and ability to form connections with others.

Do Not Forget Those You Know: Improve your relations with those who are in your life. Overcoming loneliness is not just about meeting new people. It is also about strengthening your relationships with the people already in your life.

Turn to Someone Whom You Trust: It is important to have someone in your life whom you trust and can talk to. If you do not have that, consider finding a therapist to take on that role for you. Your growth as a person will be accelerated when you can share your feelings with someone and get their feedback.

When lonely, we may find ourselves becoming jealous of those who seem to be popular. Jealousy is the topic of the next chapter.

Chapter 13:
The Emotion of Jealousy

The emotion of jealousy involves the perceived or real threat to an interpersonal relationship or something else they may have to someone else. Also, feelings of jealousy are often accompanied by other emotions, including anger, resentment, and feelings of inadequacy.

As stated earlier, jealousy is a normal emotion when there is a threat of losing something that we have to someone else. When a relationship is threatened, a healthy amount of jealousy can get us to give higher priority to our relationships.

When jealousy goes too far, it can damage a relationship, especially when the threat to the relationship is perceived rather than being an actual threat. For example, there is a big difference between me becoming jealous because I see my wife talking to another man and me feeling jealous because I have evidence of an affair. In the former, my jealousy is based on insecurity or low self-esteem. In the latter, my jealousy is tied to an actual threat and the betrayal of trust.

Categories of Jealousy

Jealousy can be divided into two main categories, normal and abnormal. Each main category has subcategories (Sheppard, 2022). They are as follows:

1. Normal Jealousy

- Rational Jealousy: Rational jealousy occurs when one has reasonable doubt that you may be losing something important to you, particularly a partner's love.
- Family Jealousy: This form of jealousy occurs within a family where one family member is jealous of another. This is often seen in sibling rivalry.

- Sexual Jealousy: When there is a concern that a partner has been unfaithful, it may lead to sexual jealousy.
- Romantic Jealousy: Romantic jealousy occurs in a romantic relationship when there is a perceived or real threat that one of the partners may be interested in someone else.
- Power Jealousy: This kind of jealousy results from personal insecurity and is triggered when someone has something you desire. An example of this is a co-worker who is promoted to a position you want.

2. Abnormal Jealousy

Pathological Jealousy: Pathological jealousy presents controlling and manipulative behavior or extreme insecurity. This form of jealousy is often based on irrational fears and may express mental disorders like schizophrenia, obsessive-compulsive disorder, or anxiety disorder.

A study (Staloch, 2022) that included heterosexual romantically involved couples revealed that men tend to feel jealous of others' dominance while being more concerned about their partners being sexually involved with someone else. Women, on the other hand, were more jealous of the attractiveness of others while being more concerned about their partner's emotional infidelity.

What Is the Difference Between Jealousy and Envy?

The emotions of jealousy and envy are often confused with each other, but they are separate emotions. While jealousy involves the fear that a partner may be attracted to someone else, envy involves wanting what someone else has.

However, both jealousy and envy share a common root cause, insecurity. The jealous person will be insecure about their relationship, while the envious person will be insecure about themselves. Also, jealousy often leads to resentment and anger, while envy often motivates a person to want to change. Finally, jealousy is based on a feeling of rivalry, while envy is rooted in comparing oneself with others.

How Jealousy Ruins Relationships

Jealousy in a relationship can be manifested in the following ways:

- Acting obsessive
- Criticizing
- Fault finding
- Blaming
- Feeling distrust
- Being overprotective or suspicious
- Experiencing a quick temper
- Verbally abusing

These behaviors can destroy a relationship as well as fuel further distrust. A person may be jealous because they perceive that their partner is showing interest in someone else. However, their perception may not be accurate, but they will engage in these destructive behaviors. It is these behaviors that cause the relationship to end.

How Jealousy Affects the Body

When we allow jealousy to get out of hand, it cannot only damage our relationships; it can also damage us. The following are ways in which jealousy impacts the body:

- Stomach aches
- Headaches
- Chest pain
- High blood pressure
- Palpitation in extreme anxiety
- Weight gain or loss
- Insomnia or disturbances in sleep

- Poor appetite

- Weakened immunity

How Jealousy Affects the Mind

When someone experiences intense jealousy, it may be associated with other mental health conditions, including:

- Anxiety disorders

- Attachment issues

- Borderline personality disorder (BPD)

- Depression

- Obsessive-compulsive disorder (OCD)

- Paranoia

- Psychosis

- Schizophrenia

If you experience extreme jealousy, it is recommended that you speak to a mental health professional, as not dealing with it can prevent you from functioning normally in your life.

How to Deal With Jealousy

If you experience intense levels of jealousy or it interrupts your life, you should see a mental health professional. Treatments for jealousy include:

Psychotherapy: Two forms of psychotherapy are effective in overcoming jealousy: cognitive behavioral therapy (CBT) and cognitive-analytic therapy (CAT). Both therapies will help you change how you view things to empower yourself and your relationship.

Medication: Medication is sometimes used when jealousy stems from other mental disorders, such as anxiety or depression.

When experiencing extreme jealousy, it is important to address it with a mental health professional. If not addressed, it may lead to abuse or paranoia.

How to Cope With Jealousy

The following are suggestions for how you can cope with jealousy:

Stand Up to Your Fears: Jealousy is normally caused by insecurity or a poor self-image. Your insecurity or poor self-image is not who you are unless you allow them to define you. Determine what your fears are and acknowledge that they exist, then challenge their validity. Do you have evidence to give you a reason to be jealous, or are your jealous feelings being fueled by fears or unproven beliefs? By determining if your fears can be substantiated, you can then question the validity of your fears.

Know the Expectations of the Relationship: It is important that you and your partner share the expectations that you have for the relationship. If you do not know each other's expectations, how can you support each other? Discuss with each other your expectations. If there is a disagreement in any of your expectations, work together to find a compromise that both of you can live with.

Cultivate an Attitude of Gratitude: When focused on our problems, we frequently lose sight of everything we can be grateful for. You can even learn to be grateful for feeling jealous if it makes you stronger and happier.

Remain Honest and Open: To have a successful relationship, you need successful communication. If you are feeling jealous, you must share your feelings with your partner without accusing or blaming them. Take responsibility by using the "I statement." An example of this is, "I am feeling jealous, and I need to talk to you about this." When talking about it, your goal should be that the conversation leads to both of you building trust in each other.

Practice Mindfulness: By practicing mindfulness, you will develop greater awareness of your thoughts and feelings without judgment. You then can deal with them without getting caught up in them.

As mentioned earlier, jealousy is often confused with envy, which is the topic of the next chapter.

Chapter 14:
The Emotion of Envy

T he emotion of envy can be described as negative feelings that occur due to the possessions or advantages that another person has, which you desire. As mentioned earlier, envy differs from jealousy in that jealousy is the concern or fear that someone else will take something you believe you own.

Envy is an emotion that we all experience from time to time, and it is relatively harmless. However, when envy gets out of hand, it can be harmful to your emotional well-being and relationships. While most people can regulate the emotion of envy, some have difficulty managing it. If you have a problem with envy, the first thing to do is to learn how to handle it.

What Envy Looks Like

The following are behaviors that are exhibited by people who have issues with envy:

- Feeling threatened by other people's success, which may take the form of not celebrating their achievements

- Showing pleasure when others experience failure or setbacks

- Spending a lot of time judging or scrutinizing what others are doing

- Consistently downplaying the success of others

- Being insincere in their compliments of others

- Spreading rumors about others

It should be noted that someone can have issues with envy but not engage in any of these behaviors.

Conditions That Create Envy

The following are some of the conditions or causes that may lead to feelings of envy:

- A person believes that another has possessions or advantages they want for themselves
- The belief that to be considered worthy, one needs continuous success or accumulation of material goods
- They need to constantly compare themselves to others as it relates to success
- The belief that success is scarce or limited and that one needs to compete with others to attain it

These causes are likely subconscious, so the person may not know they have an issue.

How Unhealthy Envy Affects Us

When an individual experiences envy at an unhealthy level, it can affect them emotionally by creating ongoing stress. Further, it is damaging to relationships. If you are in a relationship with someone who cannot manage their envy, you must set personal boundaries for yourself. When setting personal boundaries, do the following:

Identify How Their Behavior Has Impacted You: If you realize that someone envies you, you have been impacted by their behavior. Identify how their behaviors have affected you. How does it make you feel?

Establish Your Boundaries: After you realize how the other person's behavior makes you feel, establish boundaries for yourself. You can determine your boundary needs by asking yourself, "What do I need to happen to feel safe emotionally."

Communicate Your Boundaries: After you have defined your boundaries, you need to communicate them to the other person. When communicating your boundaries, be clear and specific. Also, avoid blaming the other person. Instead, use "I Statements," such as

"I feel uncomfortable when you ..." followed by "What I need from you is ..."

Enforce Your Boundaries: Boundaries are useless unless you enforce them. Also, they need to be enforced consistently. If the other person violates your boundaries, let them know. If they continue to violate your boundaries, give them consequences. The following are examples of how to communicate your boundaries and enforce them.

> **Do not say**: "Please stop putting down my success when I am around others."

> **Do say**: "If you continue to put down my success when others are around, I will stop inviting you to my events."

Also, this method of setting boundaries can be used for situations where the other person's behavior negatively affects you.

Ways to Express Healthy Envy

The following are ways that you can express envy in a positive way that supports not only others but you:

Identify the Feeling: Next time you experience yourself becoming envious, take a moment to identify the feeling it brings up in you. Also, note the following:

- What happened to cause you to feel triggered by this emotion? What was the situation? Who was involved?

- What would you have to believe to feel this way?

Asking these questions will give you greater clarity about what is behind your feelings.

Begin to Appreciate Your Life: Start taking stock of what you can appreciate about your life. When a person has excess envy, it often blinds them from the good things they already have in their life.

Focus on Compassion: We are often envious of others without realizing that they may be suffering from their challenges. Focus on being compassionate toward others for what they may be going through will remove your focus on feeling envy.

A Driver of Self-Improvement: Make your envy a constructive force by using it to drive you toward developing yourself to become the person you want to be. Also, you can take note of what makes you envious of others and work on improving yourself in that area.

Speaking of self-improvement, one reason we do not try to improve ourselves is the fear of failure, which is the topic of the next chapter.

Chapter 15:
The Emotion of Failure

I t is human nature to want to avoid failure. The ultimate reason is that we want to avoid experiencing feelings of failure, which can be painful. As a result, we often go to great lengths to avoid experiencing it.

Other factors may contribute to that unpleasant feeling when we feel we have failed. Some of those factors include:

- A sense of hopelessness

- Anxiety

- Depression

- Feelings of helplessness

- Lack of supportive relationships

- Low self-esteem

- Making comparisons with others

- Poor self-concept

- Negative self-talk

- Unrealistic expectations

As with any emotion, it is important to separate yourself from this emotion. The emotions we experience are not who we are; they do not define us. Rather, we experience emotions, which are a form of energy. Because of this, there are things that we can do to deal with this emotion.

By learning how to deal with feelings of failure, you can minimize the fear associated with it so that you can move forward and be better for it. It is also helpful to remember that failure is part of the human condition, as everyone fails at some point in their lives.

How Failure Can Affect Your Life

The feeling of failure can be fleeting or last for prolonged periods. Losing in competitive sports may be one thing, while a relationship break-up or the closing of your business can be devastating. Regardless of the reason for your sense of failure, it can seriously impact your life if you internalize it. Holding on to feelings of failure can manifest as feelings of sadness, depression, guilt, shame, and anxiety.

These emotions can become part of your internal dialogue where you tell yourself things like:

- "I will never succeed."

- "I always screw things up."

- "I am not good enough."

- "I am a loser."

These voices become part of your inner critic, that part of your mind that makes you feel like you are not good enough. Your inner critic leads to self-doubt and a lack of confidence. If this thinking continues, it can lead to a fear of failure and depression.

Ways to Cope With Failure

Though failure is often seen as a negative, it also has a positive aspect. Failure can be seen as a teaching moment where we learn things about ourselves that will propel us forward to a happier life. For this to occur, learning how to cope with failure is important. The following are suggestions:

Embrace the Pain: Though it may seem counterintuitive, one of the best ways to overcome feelings of failure is to embrace the pain. Research demonstrates that getting in touch with the pain of failure is more motivating than it is to think about your failure (Morin, 2022).

A reason for this is that when thinking about failure, we tend to come up with excuses for failing. When we embrace the feelings of failure, we remove ourselves from our ego and get in touch with the pain. Since we are biologically wired to avoid pain, we become motivated to change.

Positive Versus Negative Coping Strategies: Just as important as embracing the pain, it is also important to catch yourself if you are attempting to reduce your pain by unhealthy methods. Attempts to distract yourself from your pain will sabotage any attempts to use your pain as a source of motivation.

Also, trying to fill the void you may be experiencing through drugs, alcohol, or food will just make things worse. These forms of distraction will create additional problems, and you will not learn to move forward with your life as if you used your pain for motivation.

Practicing healthy coping skills will help you deal with the pain of failure and benefit you long-term. Healthy coping skills include:

- Meditating
- Exercising
- Deep breathing
- Going for a walk
- Playing with your pet
- Being in nature
- Calling a friend

If you use unhealthy coping skills to remove yourself from your pain, list healthy coping skills that you can use instead and post them in a prominent place as a reminder.

Identify Your Irrational Beliefs: We all have irrational beliefs about different aspects of our lives. Irrational beliefs are beliefs that are distorted and that do not reflect reality. Because of this, these beliefs disempower us. Because we accept our beliefs as being the truth, we do not question them. Failure is one of those aspects of our lives for which we hold irrational beliefs. Examples of irrational beliefs include:

- "I always fail."

- "I will never figure it out."

- "I am a failure."

- "I do not have what it takes to succeed."

Reframe Your Irrational Beliefs: A 2016 study demonstrated that holding positive beliefs was a determining factor in one's resiliency after experiencing emotional distress due to failure. Instead of seeing themselves as failures, participants of the study viewed failure as being something specific and outside themselves rather than something wrong with them.

Instead of thinking that your situation is hopeless, reframe your thinking. Reframing means putting a positive but realistic spin on your thinking. It is like seeing the "glass half-full rather than half-empty." In other words, reframing is optimistic thinking. Examples of reframed beliefs include:

- "Failure is part of the process when taking on a challenging task."

- "Failure is my teacher."

- "Failure is what causes me to expand my understanding."

Reframe your irrational beliefs and use them as affirmations to remind yourself each day that you are on the right path and that you will bounce back.

Take Responsibility for Your Abilities: While it is important to not define yourself by your failures, taking a level of responsibility for them is important. Blaming yourself is no help, but neither is blaming others or unforeseen circumstances. Rather than make excuses, seek to understand what happened so that you can take a different approach next time.

Create a Plan: When it comes to failure, identify what went wrong, learn from it, and move forward. To move forward, you need a plan.

Create a plan for how you will approach your goal differently based on what you learned from your mistakes in the past.

Get Ready to Jump Into the Flames: Most of us have spent our lives trying to avoid failure. The last thing we want to do is experience pain. This chapter was about how to view failure constructively. Now it is time to put what you learned into practice.

To succeed in anything great, you must risk failure, which means moving beyond your comfort zone. Put yourself in situations that you avoided doing in the past because you were afraid of failing. The more you do this, the more your fear of failure will diminish.

Besides the fear of failure, resentment is also an emotion that can prevent us from taking positive action. Resentment is the topic of the next chapter.

Chapter 16:
The Emotion of Resentment

Resentment is the unpleasant feeling experienced when one believes they were mistreated or wronged by another. Frustrations and disappointments are a normal part of life. When these emotions accumulate, it leads to resentment. Resentment can be toxic to a relationship as it erodes love and trust. If resentment is not managed, it can permanently damage a relationship.

Resentment is a manifestation of anger rather than a pure emotion. We may become angry when our expectations of a relationship are not realized. When our anger makes us feel that a situation is unjust, it is transformed into resentment.

Resentment Versus Other Emotions

Other emotions are commonly mistaken for resentment. The following is a breakdown of how resentment differs from other emotions:

Resentment Versus Envy

When I was much younger, I worked at a job where there were co-workers who worked harder than I did. These individuals received a lot of recognition from management. I was envious of them.

On the other hand, some co-workers put in the same effort that I did and received more recognition than I did. I felt resentful toward them. I never felt resentful toward the higher-performing employees because I believed they deserved it. On the other hand, I felt resentful toward the other employees because I felt it was unfair.

Resentment Versus Anger

Resentment is a form of anger. However, it is more specific. We experience anger when we feel that our boundaries have been violated or our expectations were unmet. Resentment is expressed when the situation involves unfairness.

Also, anger is a natural response to something that we find displeasing. On the other hand, resentment involves repeatedly reviewing the memories of a hurtful situation. Resentment is connected to anger in that anger that is allowed to persist may turn into resentment. Finally, anger can be beneficial because it can cause us to act. On the other hand, resentment offers no positive outcomes.

Resentment and Opposing Emotions

Just as there are emotions that are confusing for resentment, there are also emotions that are the direct opposite. These emotions are a valuable ally when trying to overcome feelings of resentment, as resentment cannot exist when these emotions are present.

Resentment Versus Forgiveness

While resentment is holding on to the feeling of injustice, forgiveness is letting go of the feeling of injustice. It is not that forgiveness turns a blind eye to the injustice or does not acknowledge what happened. Rather, forgiveness releases this potentially toxic energy so that healing can take place. This provides the opportunity for a new understanding between individuals that benefits both.

Resentment Versus Gratitude

When we feel resentment, we have ill feelings for another as we believe that they deprived us of our happiness. While this feeling can be legitimate, resentment can also prevent us from seeing the larger picture. Sometimes we overlook the other person's motives and fail to realize that their actions were not intentional. Because our perceptions of the other person may be limited, we deprive ourselves of happiness by being resentful.

By focusing on what we are grateful for, we can move beyond the tunnel vision that resentment creates and gain clarity in our thinking.

The Symptoms of Resentment

The feelings of resentment are normally temporary. However, there are times when we may hold on to resentment, which may lead to the following symptoms:

Recurring Feelings of Negativity: These are the reoccurring negative emotions toward people or situations you believe are responsible for your unhappiness. These emotions may include:

- Anger

- Frustration

- Hostility

- Bitterness

- Hard feelings

- Uneasiness

You Cannot Stop Thinking About It: When strong resentment exists, it causes one to keep thinking about the situation that triggered these feelings. Some continue to replay this toxic thinking for years.

Remorseful or Regretful Feelings: Some individuals may experience remorse or regret for their remorseful feelings and blame themselves for what happened in the past. They may wish that they handled things differently.

Avoidance or Fear: Holding on to resentment can lead to the triggering of painful memories. A person may avoid certain situations or people because they bring up these memories.

Unhealthy Relationships: Resentment can follow you through relationships. The source of resentment may no longer be in your life. However, the behaviors of holding grudges, acting out, or being passive-aggressive may live on.

Resentment and Relationships

When there is resentment in a relationship, it affects each partner differently, depending on which partner is harboring resentment. The partner who is harboring resentment may do the following:

- Have unexpected expressions of anger

- Lack empathy for their loved ones

- Emotionally withdraw from their partner

The partner who is not harboring resentment may feel anxious about the relationship. Also, they may be confused about why their partner is expressing resentment. As a result, they respond with defensiveness.

How Resentment Shows Up in a Relationship

There is no hard and fast rule as to how resentment shows up in a relationship, as each person and each relationship is different. That said, the following are the most common ways that resentment shows up in a relationship:

When You Are the Partner Who Is Resentful

- Behaving passive-aggressively or sarcastically toward your partner

- Feeling agitated when you are with your partner

- Feeling like you want to leave the relationship

- Showing a lack of empathy toward your partner

- A decline in sex or intimacy

- Feelings of disappointment or disgust toward your partner

- Frequently making complaints about your partner when talking to your friends

When Your Partner is Resentful Toward You

- You feel distant from your partner

- You feel anxious about the relationship

- You experience increased arguing and are confused as to why it is happening

- You feel ignored and that your opinion is not important

How to Avoid Resentment From Taking Over

If you are experiencing resentment in your relationship, the following are ways that you can help improve the situation:

Do Not Let Any Relationship Issues Slip By: Do not let any arguments go unresolved. With each issue that arises, work with your partner to find a resolution that you both can agree to.

Learn How to Communicate Your Feelings More Effectively: A major cause of resentment in relationships is the inability to communicate how you feel without judging or blaming your partner. Learn to express your feelings assertively.

Additionally, it is important that you are clear and direct as to what is bothering you. If you can communicate the problem, you will minimize the risk of resentment.

Maintain Realistic Expectations: When we enter a relationship, we often expect how it will progress. When those expectations are not met, we become disappointed. There are certain expectations, such as personal boundaries, which we should always respect. Personal boundaries are the rules we need to set for ourselves that allow us to feel emotionally safe.

However, other expectations are not tied to our boundaries. These rules are our preferences. Everyone has different preferences, so it is okay if you and your partner have different preferences. Do not let a difference in your preferences develop into resentment.

In the next chapter, we will discuss a feeling that can be the product of any of the emotions that are discussed in this book, which is the feeling of overwhelm.

Chapter 17:
The Emotion of Overwhelm

The feeling of being overwhelmed occurs when the number of thoughts and emotions we experience is more than we can process. In other words, we feel like more is happening than we can handle. All of us experience overwhelm at one point or another.

The stress we experience from being overwhelmed can be beneficial if it causes us to step up our game. This emotion becomes a problem when it becomes chronic. When this happens, it can hurt our mental and physical health.

Signs That You May Be Overwhelmed

Being chronically overwhelmed can lead to the following symptoms:

Distorted Thinking: You see the problem being bigger than it is while doubting your ability to deal with it.

You Freeze: You feel paralyzed due to the freeze response. The mind and body have the "fight and flight" response, which is a survival mechanism. When there is a perceived threat, our mind and body kick into high alert by preparing to fight or flee.

Many do not realize there is another component to the "fight and flight" response. That component is freezing. When we feel overwhelmed, we freeze mentally. When this occurs, even doing simple things may seem difficult.

Disproportionate Response: You respond to minor stressors by overreacting. For example, you panic when you are running late for an appointment.

Withdrawal: You isolate yourself from others.

Pessimism: You feel hopeless about overcoming the situation.

Changes in Mood: You experience mood swings where you frequently cry and feel anxious, angry, or irritable.

Brain Fatigue: You are easily confused and have problems concentrating or making decisions.

Physical Symptoms:

- Headaches
- Fatigue
- Dizziness
- Cramps
- Upset stomach
- Aches and pains

Causes of Overwhelm

Feeling overwhelmed can be caused by precipitating stressors such as unanticipated events, mental health challenges, or a lack of coping skills. Additionally, the accumulation of small stressors can also lead to feeling this way. Some examples of precipitating stressors include:

- The death of a loved one
- A stressful work environment or being overworked
- Strains in a relationship or a breakup
- Financial struggles
- Health problems
- Traumatic events
- Political or environmental issues
- Major changes in life
- Mental health challenges such as anxiety, depression, or post-traumatic stress disorder

How to Cope With Overwhelm

The following are strategies that can help you cope when you feel overwhelmed:

Change Your Outlook: How we look at things determines how we feel about them. If you change your perspective, you will feel differently. If you ever experience a situation where someone talked to you and made you feel better, it was because they offered you a different point of view that you were not considering at the time. Learn to look at things in an empowering but realistic way, and you will be less likely to become overwhelmed.

Challenge Your Beliefs: When we feel overwhelmed, we focus on the negative and allow distorted thinking to attract our attention. Quite often, our thoughts are about what others will think about us if they ever find out about what we are going through. This kind of thinking often accompanies situations like relationship break-ups.

If you are experiencing thoughts consuming you, identify each one and challenge it by putting it into the light of reality. Look for any evidence that would support your thinking. If you cannot find evidence to support your thinking, your fears may be more imagined than real. Also, writing down your thoughts is valuable for clarifying whether they make sense.

Find Support: Reach out to others such as family, friends, or colleagues. You can join a support group if you do not have anyone. Let these people know what you are going through and see if they can offer you a different perspective.

Practice Mindfulness: Practicing mindfulness is a powerful way of overcoming overwhelm for several reasons. First, you will learn not to make judgments about what you are experiencing. Second, you learn to recognize your thoughts and emotions without personalizing them. Doing these things will calm your mind and make you aware of the present moment rather than focusing on the future or the past.

Find a Therapist: Going to therapy can help you identify the causes of your overwhelm, examine the meaning you give them, and develop more empowering ways to address them. You will also learn coping skills.

When we feel overwhelmed, it may lead to feelings of inadequacy, which is the topic of the next chapter.

Chapter 18:
The Emotion of Inadequacy

A person may doubt themselves or dwell on their past mistakes, leading them to develop negative beliefs about themselves. These negative beliefs will create negative feelings. The combination of negative beliefs and negative feelings creates the feeling of inadequacy. For this reason, feelings of inadequacy are mentally and emotionally based.

When feelings of inadequacy last long-term, it negatively impacts one's self-confidence. The feelings of inadequacy lead to having negative expectations for situational outcomes.

While many factors can contribute to feelings of inadequacy, some of the more common ones include:

Focusing on the Past: Focusing on our past mistakes makes having hope for the future difficult. Focusing on past mistakes creates negative feelings, influencing how we think about the future.

Isolation: When we surround ourselves with others, it increases the odds that we will experience feelings of validation, which is impossible if we withdraw from others. By withdrawing from others, we become isolated, and our only reference to our self-worth is our distorted thinking.

Ignoring Hidden Benefits: When we focus on the negative aspects of our past performances, we judge them as failures. However, we also overlook the important lessons we could learn from them, which we could apply in the future.

Not Being Realistic: We are bound to feel disappointed when we have unrealistic expectations of ourselves. Instead of seeing that we had set the bar too high, we blame ourselves.

Your Experience of Childhood: When a person feels inadequate during childhood, it often spills over into adulthood. When children feel unloved or unsafe, they often feel inadequate. As they grow older, they doubt their value.

Physical Appearance and Functions: Feeling inferior can be linked to physical appearance, which may include:

- Physical disfigurements for abnormalities
- Weight issues
- Speech impediments

Social and Economic Challenges: Coming from a background of social or economic disadvantages may lead to feelings of inadequacy. Examples of how this may be experienced include:

- The person has the least financial resources among their friends or those they associate with
- They constantly need to reach out to family or friends for financial assistance, which impacts their self-worth
- Being unable to find employment
- Being unable to support their family
- Any form of public embarrassment

Do You Have an Inferiority Complex?

The following are signs that you may have an inferiority complex:

- You have low self-esteem
- You overthink the compliments and criticisms that you receive
- You are constantly looking for validation from others
- You withdraw socially from others
- You put others down to feel better about yourself
- You avoid competitive events to avoid being compared with others

The Impact of Having an Inferiority Complex

When a person has an inferiority complex, it can impact every aspect of their life. The following are some of the more harmful ways that having an inferiority complex can manifest:

Higher Incidence of Addictions: Constantly feeling inferior to others can be taxing, so there is a higher incidence of drug or alcohol addictions, which are used as a way to cope with negative feelings. In turn, addictions lead to further negative feelings. Addictions may also lead to further health problems.

Depression: Having a prevailing attitude that you are not good enough can be tiring. You are constantly second-guessing yourself, which can affect your mental health. One of the impacts on mental health is depression.

Poor Quality of Life: Feeling inferior creates additional stress whenever you compare yourself to others. This kind of comparison can show up both socially and professionally. Examples of this include:

- The person with the inferiority complex is asked questions by family or loved ones regarding their life status or achievements
- The person with the inferiority complex compares themselves to their co-workers, leading to losing focus on job responsibilities

Coping With Feelings of Inadequacy

If you feel inadequate, you believe that others are better than you. The reason for this is that this is where your focus is. Whatever we focus on becomes our experience. You are not focusing on your uniqueness as an individual with your unique strengths and abilities. The following are ways to cope with feelings of inadequacy and recognize those strengths and abilities.

Seek Therapy: A therapist can assist you in identifying the specific reasons why you feel inadequate and help you develop more empowering beliefs about yourself. In addition, they can help you develop your coping and problem-solving skills. These approaches will build your confidence and help you better appreciate yourself.

Maintain a Journal: Keep a journal and record your thoughts daily. In writing out your thoughts, you will gain greater clarity in your thinking and the triggering events that brought about your thinking. With greater clarity, you will begin to recognize the reasons why you are worthy of love and respect.

Make Use of Affirmations: Affirmations are statements of empowerment that we tell ourselves. Repeating affirmations with conviction creates a new focal point for our attention instead of our negative thinking. When you continuously use affirmations, they become established in your belief system.

Each time you repeat an affirmation, you strengthen a positive belief about yourself. In this way, you are doing the reverse of what you normally do: continuously repeating negative thoughts about yourself. When you repeat affirmations, you are rewiring your brain to believe in the positive aspects of yourself.

When using affirmations, choose affirmations that resonate or are meaningful to you. Also, say them with emotion, as you mean it. When you first start repeating affirmations, it may seem like you are just repeating words. Do not worry about this, as this is normal. Keep repeating your affirmations daily, as it takes about a month of consistent repeating before changes in how you feel will become noticeable.

In the next chapter, you will learn about another feeling state that is a product of one of the negative emotions. That feeling state is emptiness.

Chapter 19:
The Emotion of Emptiness

Sometimes we feel empty; however, this feeling is a secondary emotion. Something else lies beneath this feeling that needs to be uncovered to resolve the emptiness feeling. Often, the empty feeling resolves itself after a short period. When this feeling is prolonged, it may point to a cognitive disorder, and professional help may be needed.

How Emptiness Is Experienced

The feeling of emptiness can be experienced differently by each person. If you are feeling emptiness, you may feel unmotivated, lonely, or confused about your life.

Causes for Feeling Empty

There are numerous reasons why one may feel empty. Such reasons can range from hormonal changes to losing a relationship or employment. However, here are some common causes for feeling empty:

Self-Reflection: Temporary feelings of emptiness often arise when a situation causes you to self-reflect on your life. You may experience a life change or unexpected event that causes you to self-reflect, which can lead to feeling empty. This sense of emptiness is a benefit in that it quiets your mental noise so that greater attention can be given to understanding your situation.

Losing Your Connection With Yourself: Many of us live hectic lives that are full of commitments and deadlines. We may also spend so much time caring for others that we forget to care for ourselves. Whenever we cannot connect with ourselves, meaning our thoughts and feelings, due to the demands of others, we may experience feelings of emptiness. It is for this reason that practicing self-care is so important.

An Unresolved Past: Another cause of emptiness is that we may not have fully grieved a loss we experienced in the past. Unresolved pains from the past, as far back as childhood, still have their energies percolating within us. Because we did not go through the grieving process, their energies continue to appear.

When there is a loss in our lives, be it the death of a loved one or a trauma from childhood, it is important to go through the grieving process so those energies can be expressed and released. The best way to do this is to talk to someone you can trust.

The Absence of Self-Care: Regardless of the cause of our emotional suffering, the most important way to deal with it is through self-care. What prevents us from practicing self-care comes down to three main reasons:

- We feel that it is not important.

- We focus too much on the needs of others and not enough on ourselves.

- We are not attuned to our needs.

Lack of Meaningful Relationships: Studies at Harvard Medical School show that healthy relationships are the most influential aspect of the human experience (Mineo, 2017). It is not the quantity of our relationships but their quality. Healthy relationships create emotional intimacy, active listening, support, and companionship. When these qualities are missing from our lives, it may lead to empty feelings, not to mention loneliness.

Ways to Cope With Feelings of Emptiness

If feelings of emptiness have persisted beyond a few weeks, it is recommended that you see a mental health professional who can help guide you in working through your feelings and identifying their cause. You then will be able to resolve these feelings. For those who are experiencing feelings of emptiness for short periods, the following are suggestions:

Give Acknowledgment: Acknowledge what you feel whether it is emptiness or any other emotion. This is the first step to dealing with this negative emotion. Besides acknowledging these feelings, be gentle with yourself and do not judge yourself or your feelings.

Many of us have learned to dismiss our feelings, which is a mistake. By acknowledging your feelings, you are accepting their existence, allowing you to address them. Also, by acknowledging your feelings, you are showing compassion for yourself. If, when acknowledging your feelings, you discover that they are due to a loss, you need to grieve that loss.

Devote Time to Yourself: Each day, regardless of how busy you are, devote some time to yourself. However, devoting time to yourself does not necessarily mean partying or watching television. Rather, devote time to be with yourself and engage in self-reflection. Look within and explore your dreams, desires, and fears. Excellent ways to do this are through meditation or journaling.

Check In With Your Feelings: Each day, take five minutes where you just explore your feelings. Notice what you are experiencing emotionally at this time. Emotions that you may identify include:

- Feeling bored
- Feeling distracted
- Feeling curious
- Feeling numb

By doing this daily, you will gain greater awareness of your feelings, which will help you determine why you feel empty.

Investigate the Feeling of Emptiness: Using a journal, write about what you are experiencing when you feel empty. You can do this by asking yourself questions such as:

- Am I passing judgment on myself?
- Am I comparing myself to other people?

- Do I have positive thoughts about myself, or am I being critical of myself?

- In my relationships, are my feelings being honored?

- Am I expressing my feelings in my relationships, or am I denying them?

- Am I practicing self-care for both my mental and physical needs?

- Am I engaging in addictive behaviors to avoid experiencing my feelings?

- Am I neglecting my needs while focusing on the needs of others?

- Am I trying to prove something to myself or other people?

- Are there things I blame myself for that are out of my control?

- Are there things I feel guilty about that are out of my control?

- Am I treating myself with the kind of compassion that I would treat a friend or a loved one?

- Am I standing up for my decisions and respecting my personal beliefs?

Reach Out to Others: After you have taken time to be alone and explore your feelings, reach out to others. By connecting with others, you will feel better. If you can share with them what you are feeling, that would be even better.

Engage in Self-Care: When feeling empty, you may neglect taking care of yourself, making things worse. Commit to self-care daily by exercising, eating healthfully, and getting plenty of sleep. Also, find ways to express your feelings, such as talking to someone or journaling.

Acknowledge Yourself: We are all doing the best that we can with what we know. The thing that we are all striving for is to feel happy, while self-knowledge varies with each person. The more we understand how we treat ourselves and its impact on how we feel, the more likely we will become happy.

Seek Help: Sometimes we struggle to feel better, and we cannot rise above our feelings of emptiness. These are the times when we need to realize that we cannot do it on our own and that there is no shame in that. This is the point when it is highly recommended that you see a mental health professional to talk to. Talking to a therapist can empower you to make the changes needed to feel again and enjoy your life.

Your Voice Matters

Dear Reader,

I hope that this book has offered you valuable insights and practical strategies to navigate your emotional landscape. Your journey toward inner peace is unique and valuable, and I am grateful to have been a part of it through this book.

Your perspective and experiences are important, and sharing them can make a significant difference. By taking a moment to write an honest review on Amazon, you help others who are seeking ways to manage their emotions find this resource. You contribute to a wider conversation about emotional health, stress, and personal growth, and your experiences can offer comfort and guidance to others on a similar journey.

As an author, your feedback is deeply valuable to me. It illuminates the impact of my work and guides me as I continue to write and explore these important topics. Please consider sharing your thoughts on Amazon when you have a moment.

Scan to leave a review

I look forward to reading your honest review, and I am grateful for your time and engagement. Thank you for joining me in this journey toward managing negative emotions and achieving inner peace.

Sincerely,

Andrew Tenny

Conclusion

If we were to look from the higher consciousness perspective, it would be evident that there are neither good nor bad emotions; there is just energy. We experience this energy as being good or bad because we are socialized to believe this. In this way, emotions are like cows.

In Western societies, cows are widely used as a source of food. The cow is seen as sacred in India, and no one would dare harm it. The cow is neither a source of food nor sacred; it is just a cow. It is we who project our interpretation of its value onto it.

Similarly, we have learned to identify emotions as being positive or negative. Just as a cow is a cow, an emotion is just an emotion, and it is an inherent aspect of our lives. Though emotions are an inherent aspect of your life, they do not define who you are as a person.

You can think of your relationship with emotions as the relationship between the clouds and the sky. On some days, the sky is filled with clouds, while on other days, they are absent. Whether the sky is cloudy or clear, the sky remains the sky. You are to the sky as emotions are to the clouds. They, too, will sometimes hang around while other times they will transverse the skies of your awareness.

Learn to accept the negative emotions that enter the skies of your awareness and learn from them the message they are sending. All emotions are valuable if we learn to embrace and learn from their existence.

The mind and body are amazing expressions of life's wisdom. Together they perform countless functions and processes that allow us to experience life. Additionally, life's wisdom permeates the mind and body to keep it in a balanced state where these functions and processes can perform at an optimal level.

How we treat the mind and body determines if this balanced state can be maintained or if it is allowed to go off balance.

Unfortunately, most of us have lost our connection with the wisdom that occupies the mind-body apparatus. We have allowed negative thinking and the stresses of our modern society to distract us from the essential aspects of who we are. We have come to disdain, avoid, or suppress the emotions that we deem as negative in hopes of finding a shortcut to happiness rather than learning from them.

This book has provided information on various negative emotions and how to cope with them. In truth, all this information could have been conveyed in less than a page if we had a greater understanding of emotions' role in our lives. If I had only one page to convey this message, I would have written this:

Treat any emotion you experience as part of a feedback loop between you and life's intelligence. The emotions you are experiencing give you feedback as to whether you are becoming closer aligned further part from life's wisdom.

If you are learning to think compassionately toward yourself and others and living your life as though your life, and the life of others, is sacred, then you are becoming more aligned with life's wisdom. From this, you will enjoy greater emotional well-being.

On the other hand, if you are doing the opposite, you will not experience emotional well-being. The negative emotions that you are experiencing are a sign that some area of your life is not in balance. Learn to embrace your negative emotions and let them be your teacher. Go within and listen to what they have to say. Ask yourself, "What is this emotion trying to tell me?" After asking this question, remain silent and just listen. The answer will come to you if you are patient. Learning to meditate or practicing mindfulness is huge for becoming successful in this.

Also, remember that life is not perfect. We are not intended to be perfect. Nor are we intended to please others. Rather, life is about learning to appreciate the wonder that you are without any ego. Every person comes into this world with their unique gifts and talents. The more that you let your negative emotions guide you, the closer you will come to offer the world.

About the Author

Andrew Tenny, a skilled wordsmith and empathetic storyteller, is the author of the influential book, *Managing Negative Emotions*. His work is centered around promoting emotional resilience and equipping readers with practical tools to navigate the stormy seas of negative feelings.

Andrew's journey began as a young boy, who was keenly aware of the emotions swirling around him. He possessed a natural curiosity that led him to explore the labyrinth of human feelings. This curiosity was the genesis of a lifelong journey to understand the emotional complexities of the human psyche, a journey that he shares with his readers.

Andrew has spent countless hours diving into the world of psychology, neuroscience, and self-help literature, informally educating himself and gathering insights from various sources. His knack for making complex ideas accessible has been cultivated through years of thoughtful study and observation.

The catalyst for *Managing Negative Emotions* was Andrew's struggle with emotional turbulence. He learned to reframe his perspective and manage his feelings, transforming his life from a state of constant chaos to a more centered existence.

Andrew's approach to managing emotions combines a mix of mindfulness practices, cognitive restructuring techniques, and positive psychology principles. His methods have helped countless readers to navigate their emotional landscapes more effectively, and he is committed to continuing this mission.

In his free time, Andrew enjoys practicing mindfulness meditation and exploring the great outdoors. He believes in the therapeutic power of nature and often retreats to serene landscapes for inspiration and rejuvenation. He is a lover of classical music and a proud owner of a vintage vinyl collection.

References

Arias, A. J. (2020). The Neuroscience Of Sadness: A Multidisciplinary Synthesis And Collaborative Review. *Science Direct*

Biggers, A. (2018). Why Is Oxytocin Known as the 'Love Hormone'? And 11 Other FAQs. *Heatlhline*

Clarke, J. (2022). What Is Unrequited Love? *Verywell Mind*.

Cunic, A. (2023) The Psychology of Shame. *Verywell Mind*.

Dodgson, L. (2018). A Psychotherapist Says There Are 4 Types Of Shame — Here's What They Are And How They Affect Us. *Insider*

Holmes, L. (2023). What Is Mental Health? *Verywell Mind*.

Horsager-Boehrer, R. (2021). 1 in 10 dads experience postpartum depression, anxiety: How to spot the signs. UT Southwestern Medical Center.

Kammerer, A. (2019). The Scientific Underpinnings and Impacts of Shame. *Scientific American*.

Mineo, L. (2017). Genes Are Nice, But Joy Is Better. *Harvard Gazette*.

Morin, A. (2022). 10 Healthy Ways to Cope With Failure. *Verywell Mind*.

NLM (National Library of Medicine. DSM-5 Changes: Implications for Child Serious Emotional Disturbance.

Otte, C. (2011) Cognitive behavioral therapy in anxiety disorders: current state of the evidence. *PubMed Central*.

Patel, R.K. and Rose, G.M. (2022). Persistent Depressive Disorder. *PubMed Central*.

Psychology Today (2023) Anger.

Robbins, T. (N.D.) How To Overcome Fear: Unlock The Psychology Of Fear And 10 Steps To Overcome It.

Sheppard, S. (2022). What Is Jealousy? *Verywell Mind*.

Staloch, L. (2022). Jealousy May Depend On The Interplay Of Gender, Sexual Orientation, And Gender Of The Rival. *PsyPost*.

WHO (World Health Organization (2023). Depressive disorders.

Printed in Great Britain
by Amazon

36915725R00066